Redemption of the Human Spirit

Joseph Colianni

Trilogy Christian Publishers
A Wholly Owned Subsidiary of Trinity Broadcasting Network
2442 Michelle Drive
Tustin, CA 92780

For information, address Trilogy Christian Publishing
Rights Department, 2442 Michelle Drive, Tustin, Ca 92780.
Trilogy Christian Publishing/ TBN and colophon are trademarks of Trinity Broadcasting Network.
For information about special discounts for bulk purchases, please contact Trilogy Christian Publishing.
Manufactured in the United States of America
Trilogy Disclaimer: The views and content expressed in this book are those of the author and may not necessarily reflect the views and doctrine of Trilogy Christian Publishing or the Trinity Broadcasting Network.

10 9 8 7 6 5 4 3 2 1
Library of Congress Cataloging-in-Publication Data is available.
B-ISBN#: 978-1-64088-435-9
E-ISBN#: 978-1-64088-436-6

Reviews

"For a long time, Fathers have abdicated their role and have left a generation flailing, searching for purpose, affirmation, and direction. We have exposed our children to the devastation of mental-health issues and spiritual deficiency. This has left our communities broken and our world reeling in the pain of a loss of something they never knew they needed. Joseph Colianni refocuses us on the one eternal flame of purpose, direction, and value. He shows us the one who never abdicated fatherhood and stands ready to restore the wandering person. As you read through *Redemption of the Human Spirit,* your life will be made alive to purpose, and your dreams will be reawakened" (Pastor Thomas Galban, lead pastor, Risen King Church).

"Joseph Colianni, Christian author, his first book, *Redemption of the Human Spirit*, written on November 2018 is a must read book. In this book, the author's lifetime experiences give birth to a powerful testimony. His transparency opens the door for every reader to identify with the struggles of life and the pursuit of happiness.

"Regarding this theme, Mr. Colianni digs the wells of truth written in the Bible but with a revelation of its application for our time and our society. He shows us how every negative human thought and emotion has an origin. More importantly, he shows us how these negative thoughts and emotions can be resolved, allowing us to live a life in victory. Yes, we can leave a legacy of truth and understanding that transforms individuals, families, communities, and nations. I would like to see this book translated to every language so it can bless our generation and generations to come all around the world" (Adeline E. Carter, MD, prophetess and elder consultant of Word of Living Water International Church, CAGUAS, PR, and MY GOD Doer of Miracles International Church, Villalba, Puerto Rico).

"Just because you don't like the truth doesn't change the truth. Through this book and the writings of Joseph, you will begin to understand the truth that will set you free" (Pastor Isaac Friedel, Shore Christian Church).

"With honesty and personal vulnerability, this book takes you on a thought-provoking journey for absolute truth and the search for significance" (Josephine Scott, Cry of the Soul Ministry).

Contents

Acknowledgments

I would like to thank my wife, Elaine, who saw a talent in me as I would write poems that were in her estimation a gift from God and should be published (see the appendix) and also for my daughter Monica for her expertise in the editing of these words. To my pastor Thomas A. Galban who is an encouragement to me. To Evelyn Lang who is a fellow author and is the main reason this book got the exposure it needed to get here. To Pastor Norris Lopez and to all those who helped me get this work completed. To Pastor John O. Bordigon who is now in heaven and knows more about this book than any of us can know. And for my pastor Dr. Patrick J. Fiore whose ministry and leadership lead me to pursue my calling. But without the saving knowledge of Jesus Christ, I would have no idea of the value of life, and for that, I am forever grateful. Thank you all.

Introduction

In our world today where everyone has a say in the norm of the culture and where the popular opinion has undermined the truth, we are required, if not obligated, to choose a position on even the most trivial of popular social agendas. In society today, if we happen to err on a more conservative side or have opinions generated by moral principles, we are in jeopardy of losing social status, or even worse, we are in a culture that has undermined the moral of many. It seems the popular vote on who you are in today's world far outweighs the substance, integrity, and character of the individual, undermining those certain inalienable rights that were given to us from the founders of this great nation—the right to life, liberty, and the pursuit of happiness. This usurping of an individual of their God-given right to be who they are through their convictions has led to the unraveling of the human spirit—that part of us by which we determine things to be right or wrong—and has undermined the truth, the foundation of all logic.

If understanding and acting on the truth has the ability to set one free, it has to be based on reason. Without reason, the truth is in bondage to the social norm of popular opinion, a disease that is killing the body, soul, and spirit of this great nation founded on the freedom of the individual. If the soul of a nation is not founded on truth but on opinion, then like a ship without its mooring, it will be swayed by every wind of doctrine or popular ideal of those in power at the time. When the will of the people is founded on the opinion of the masses, then character and integrity are deluded in the lives of an individual and is the road to the destruction of the human spirit that drives us to pursue our dreams.

Without open-mindedness to the truth, the folly of following whatever is popular will only lead to questions without resolution. To question the truth or to deny that it has transcendent power is to promote an endless search for significance for those who oppose it and is what I fear is at the root of most of the hopelessness found in the life of even the most prominent people of today.

To deny the truth has profound complications on the conscience of an individual. It will cause us to question our character, challenge our integrity, and it forfeits our will, leading to the worthlessness and the devaluation of life, a worthless life versus a life worth living. When our conscience is violated and we transgress and compromise the value and honor of being obedient to our own principles, *a violation that is at the root of the unraveling of the truth,* we are in jeopardy of losing control of our own destiny. But the self-worth and significance of the human spirit can never bow to the popular demands of the masses without something being forfeited by the individual and is at the forefront of the battle for the soul of this nation. Without knowing our true worth and who we are, we are led like sheep to the slaughter, and without our true worth and our purpose being redeemed and bought back by the Originator, the Creator *who questions our conscience and forges the will that fights for our purpose,* we will be on an unending search for ourselves and will be able to be bought and sold in the market of social correctness.

But the original purpose that is part of who we are can never be erased.

Science and raw facts about life can never erase the conscience of a human being. When the devaluation of an individual and life in general is rooted in the ideals of others, slavery to their ideals is the end result. But the hope we all possess is a never-ending force that drives the will to survive in even the most dire circumstances and can set the captive free. This hope has to be founded on truth, or the consequences, *as we are witnessing in life today,* can be deadly. True redemption can only be attained in the reality that truth holds and knowing the consequences of denying it. When you find that what you believe in is not true, you can acknowledge it and change, deny it and rebel, or live in superficial state of mind that will someday come crashing down. In a culture with no absolutes, the loss of significance will only bring trivial excuses for the answers about life we are all looking for. Why am I here, and where do I go to promote my core beliefs that will lead to a purposeful life to be able to live out a life true to who I am? Without the things that were forfeited to the will of others and our bad choices being redeemed in light of truth, we can never reconcile our faults with our failures simply because we don't know what the truth is. So if the truth can set you free, then redemption is what can make it a reality. The spirit of America, the core beliefs of its people and her principles, is the foundation of who we are.

The things we have forfeited by not holding to what is true has found its way into the lives of all whose core convictions are challenged by whether truth can be trusted. Truth can be trusted; it is a judge unto itself. Truth can't be judged, and to do so only leads to the devaluation of life we see today. When we become a law unto ourselves is when life is valued only in what we possess in ourselves. *And we are witnessing firsthand the effects of this mind-set.* The values and principles that were pawned off for the hope in ourselves need to be bought back, redeemed by our Creator who knows their value, purpose, and intention for why we are who we are. Without the redemption of our spirit, our God consciousness, this will be a trivial pursuit. But like most today are finding out, life is not trivial, and its effects weigh heavy on the soul of this nation. It's like Jesus explained, "You must be born again of water and the spirit." The price paid for this renewing of our spirit must be purchased in spirit and in truth, not a trivial pursuit in light where we are today. Take heed not to neglect these transcendent truths about life, or before too long, it may not be so easy to welcome tomorrow.

Growing up in the Woodstock generation and experiencing the beginning of the drug culture that has permeated our society today, I know firsthand the effects mentally, physically, and emotionally of a culture that questions authority, denies the truth, and is blind to the consequences of living a life deprived of the freedom found only in sacrifice. Their mantra is "we want everything for nothing, and we want it now," a killer to what makes you an individual. And so here I am, almost seventy years old, having survived physical, emotional, and spiritual death along with a few suicide attempts as most of my peers have not. After few short stays in a psychiatric ward, I was confronted with the truth and the facts of life that really matter. This book is what I have learned by trial and error but mostly by believing that my only hope for being okay being me is by trusting in the truth found in the saving knowledge of the gospel of Jesus Christ. So please allow me to share some foundational principles that have helped me answer some of life's difficult questions and be able to work through the fear and distresses life can bring.

Thank you, and God bless you.

Chapter 1
Hopelessness

The Human Spirit

From the beginning of time, the knowledge of good and evil has governed the way to a fulfilled life by choosing to do what we know is right and good so as not to violate or compromise our core principles. This knowledge is innate in all humans. It is our spirit, *our God consciousness that we use to deem things to be right or wrong.* Without it, this world would be a dangerous place. And it's obvious to me that we are losing the knowledge of good and evil or doing our best to ignore it. The effects are obvious. It won't get any better until, as Jesus explained, we are born again of the spirit, our conscience, *the gatekeeper of the soul.* As a pretext, this spirit we all possess will be the focal point of this book. The human spirit can be redeemed but not without truth. If we ignore it, it's to our own peril. If we deny it, we will pay the price.

What Is Truth?

Have you ever wondered why there is such despair in our society and in the world today? Hopelessness and depravity has led to the unraveling of the human spirit and is the cause of most of the evil we are faced with today. Evil in the context of the human spirit is the product of a despondent and a depraved soul. Let me explain the soul in the context of this book. The soul—the mind, the will, and the emotions—differs in relation to our spirit in that the spirit or our conscience is what we use to deem things to be right or wrong, good or bad, and is present within every human heart. The spirit is what motivates us in the involvement in any relationship. It validates us as a significant part of that relationship and is the reason we say yes or no to the questions of life. And so our spirit, our soul searcher, along with our character, the traits we are born with, forms our convictions. These convictions are expressed through our body, our soul (our mind, will, and emotions), and our spirit (our conscience). These three parts—body, soul, and spirit—are what makes up the whole person. A mind totally convinced that what you believe is right and true bears witness to our convictions and brings fulfillment and significance. However, a never-ending quest for what is right and true and a cause worth standing for is not necessarily the case in our world today.

The idea that truth is relative is one of the ills that undermined the clear thinking of many today. The notion that truth cannot be absolute is baseless; in fact, if tested against itself, it falls apart. If the notion is that there is no absolute truth, then I am compelled to ask the question, "Is that absolutely true?" You can see the problem with that kind of thinking. But the fact of the matter is that this belief system leaves one empty of a solid moral conviction because if what you believe is not true, it has no merit, can be trivial, senseless, and it holds no significance. Without significance, we are like a ship without moorings at the mercy of a raging sea of opinions, left to weigh out who we are and what we are doing here. Against a tide of opinions, this search for significance influenced by a false mind-set can become the main cause of hopelessness.

In this condition with a baseless mind-set, the pleasures of life tend to be the opiate or the way to keep fulfillment and desperation far enough apart so as not to face the reality of the inevitable. At this level, the more pleasure, the less maturity, and with life and circumstance close at hand, a time of reconciliation usually comes in the form of a breakdown.

With the right set of circumstances and this baseless mind-set, dependency and eventually addiction is the next stop to an individual who is not equipped to face the challenges that life brings to all of us. These addictions are not necessarily material. As a matter of fact, their main purpose is to alleviate emotional pain or an escape from the truth.

Having a wrong belief system has consequences. Without an anchor to trust in and with no absolutes to view life as an aimless chance is—to a perceptive, intelligent individual who will calculate the trajectory of their future—a sure way to depression.

And it seems that the gifted and talented are the most susceptible to this slippery slope of false hope. I think of Robin Williams, Janis Joplin, Jimi Hendrix, Kurt Cobain, and the endless overdoses and suicides that have plagued our world in the past and even more so today.

To call these untimely deaths senseless without considering the reality of the world we live in, I think, would be disingenuous, and I cannot in good conscience allow these gifted people to die in vain.

Now I in no way condone or commend the bad choices of these individuals. But my hope and the reason I took on this task of writing this book is to expose the untruths that plague our society and especially our youth today.

Being an ex–drug user and being admitted to a mental hospital for numerous suicide attempts, my search for significance has been nothing short of a miracle, and my family will be my witness. But the values and lessons about purpose, trust, truth, life, and significance are life-saving truths. And if it's one thing I've learned about truth is that it stands alone without the need of the burden of proof and will surely set any captive free.

In the words of Dr. Henry Cloud in his book *Integrity*, "Reality is always your friend because it's never good spending time in some alternate universe to make the one we live in feel better." So as the world has lost its focus on the things that transcend, we have been led to believe that people, places, and things can fill the gaping hole in our soul. The longing for love, peace, joy, and purpose can never be found in the material world and stands in judgment of our conscience. The longing for the chance to make a difference and the acceptance from the jury of their peers can change the course of one's life. And so the Beatles were right. "Money can't buy you love." But the innocent who are judged on baseless convictions and are led to believe in something less than the truth are being deceived. The falsehood that pleasure is the direction we should take in our pursuit for true happiness is, I believe, the number one reason why the hopelessness of our society is at an epidemic proportions.

The CDC in a data brief said, "From 1999 through 2014 the age adjustable suicide rate in the USA increased 24 percent from 10.5 to 13.0 per 100,000 population, with a pace of increase after 2006. Suicide rates increased from 1999 to 2014 for both males and females for all ages 10 through 74." These are the statistics as of April 22, 2016. Please let these facts get from your head to your heart. According to these stats, if you live in a town or city of 1,000,000 or more, 7.6 suicides will occur, and no fraction of society is out for bounds for this epidemic with an age span of ten to seventy-four. This is an alarming statistic. I live in a town in northern New Jersey that many have never heard of, and I am sad to say that these stats may be lacking.

To achieve love and happiness, we as a society have to bow to things of a greater good. Transcendence is just that, bowing to a greater good. Transcendent things such as love, justice, truth, freedom of choice, and the pursuit of happiness will never lose their power in that they are bedrock to society. Transcendent things will never move, for they are anchors of truth by which the human spirit finds direction. Ignoring them is like ignoring a lighthouse; we will slam into the rocks and break into pieces, and it is my belief that our society has chosen the latter. We ignore the warnings and slam into the bedrocks of life, thinking they will move if we only ignore them.

And then instead of bowing to the greater good, today we are bowing to the baseless teaching which says that in the light of the hopelessness of human life, let us eat drink and be merry for tomorrow we die. We challenge our conscience against popular opinion and are led to believe it is a futile and worthless attempt to engage in the hope that can bring change. We are the way we are, and we can never change. There is no hope and life, and the pursuit of happiness is a lost cause. This kind of thinking leads the way to despair. And self-significance is DOA. The truth is, in life, truth and change can be your greatest ally or your worst enemy, depending on how much truth is contained in what you believe. Without truth, we are doomed to repeat the past and relive it, and in some cases, we will always be a slave to our past. In most cases, the reason why we do what we do is steeped in the mistakes of the past. And life becomes a never-ending battle for truth.

We are hopelessly broken is the unspoken message in the lives of many today. Things are the way they are and can never change. To believe this is why the statistics mentioned above continue to grow.

To err is human, but hope springs eternal. But what kind of hope does a baseless mind-set leave? Well, to hope in the human mind and in the kind of intelligence that has the power to create the wonders of the world we live in today is noble and has merit. It is astounding and is sometimes beyond belief. But they are unable to deal with the things that drive the human spirit. Learning that priceless things in life are not attainable by wealth is the lesson that every lottery winner will be forced to live out. The priceless things we all long to possess are the things money can't buy. So it seems the more we have, the greater the disappointment. When love, happiness, contentment, and gain are not attained by what we hoped would cure all of life's problems, what's left is disappointment and eventually despair.

To be able to answer the whys and the why nots with confidence is to me a far more valuable pursuit. It allows us to make our bid for the things money can't buy. We may not be able to understand the reason things happen, but we can learn to understand in part what caused them to happen. If we can't learn from our mistakes, then we are doomed to repeat the inevitable. If learning from our mistakes changes the outcome of some bad choices, then the reason for why they happen goes away. If you know the truth, the truth can and will set you free. But will you allow your mind to outweigh your will is the question.

I'm sure this sounds like a play on words, but the things that count for the most part are not tangible and can only be solved by reason and conviction, and that brings change.

To be able to attain the things in life money can't buy, there is a price, but things that are priceless can't be purchased. They must be ransomed or redeemed, which would have helped our lottery winner mentioned above. I understand many of them wound up broke with fractured families, broken relationships, and some have lost their lives. Is any of this starting to make sense?

To ransom or redeem something, you have to possess at least the amount the item is worth, and there is always a cost incurred for the time the item sat in limbo. But something believed to have no value can't be redeemed at any price just based on its own merit. Something that is valueless can't exist in that state because it has no viable function. But the truth is, worthlessness cannot live without hopelessness.

The problem is we have devoted our lives to believe we are worthless. We boast in our human frailty and expect a priceless return. Unlike tangible things that are bought and sold every day, our conscience demands an answer to life's deeper questions, or our soul—*our mind, will, and emotions*—will pay the price, sometimes physically, sometimes emotionally, and sometimes monetarily but always decisively, and the emotional pain always outweighs the physical. People will go to great heights to escape the emotional pain they are made to endure. The cutting and mutilation by people today are a self-sacrifice on their emotional alter, but the real problem is left on the shelf of the pawnshop of life.

The youth of today find no hope in life. Let me say this as a firsthand survivor, and I'm sure you'll agree that in no way are these people worthless and should not be condemned on their behavior. By believing the lie that this is the way life is and it can never change only leads to hopelessness. I may be talking to a mom or a dad out there somewhere who struggle with the whys and the why nots as it pertains to their children. Or you may have left some things on the shelf of life yourself. But I will tell you this, truth and helplessness can't be in the same box without something changing. We will talk more about this in a later chapter.

This is precisely the sad state of affairs we are in today. Think about it, in a world where truth is relative, who would not trade or sell something that seems worthless and intangible for something that gives instant gratification? Sounds good, right? It's the lie of the century. To be queen for a day and a slave again tomorrow destroys character. Any valuable traits you have been given by your Creator are thrown to the dogs.

So in the soul market of today, drugs, entertainment, possessions, food and drink, and yes, even yourself are bringing the highest prices.

The cost is the soul of a nation and even the world one person at a time, and it's the worst trade deal in the history of mankind. We are trading the priceless for the worthless, and injustice is served as a due payment. Does anyone realize the effects that this kind of belief has on those who are longing for hope and change? When we are in bondage to our own beliefs, truth is the antidote for the wayward soul.

Any parent who has lost a child can know the price of this trade, and the costs involved are far greater than most of us can imagine. Please forgive me for putting this in marketable terms; it is just to bring out a point.

I am sure they understand more than most of us that you cannot put a price on a human life. Yet it seems we have no control over what society is teaching about the truth. But if given the truth, would people, young and old, make the right decisions?

Well, put in true context as it fits in the tensions of this subject. If I describe it as life or death, I think we can agree that my assessment will be accurate. I don't know of any person being sick or even terminal who would not welcome a cure. I guess the question then is, can truth really set you free? Again this will be covered in a latter chapter.

Faults

The second cause of hopelessness we will cover is faults. Anyone lacking any? Faults, however, have something called *blame* attached to them. For the most part, faults are mistakes. And people both young and old make mistakes. Depending on their level of maturity and responsibility, the costs vary. A two-year-old can't be blamed for spilt milk, but an adult who neglects putting the cap on the milk container assumes responsibility. That means it was a mistake and shouldn't be repeated. If the adult neglects capping the milk a second time, there is waste and loss. It is no longer a mistake; it becomes a fault. Because there was waste without the title *fault* and without a good measure of blame, these people never mature. So good measure is key. Because if the blame becomes greater than the wrong, the chance that this individual will learn diminishes. Actually, if the blame is greater the offense, they tend to take on or become part of the problem. Being able to distinguish between a mistake and a fault is a great parenting tool. The problem is it's seldom the case, and the parent imparts blame and leads their children to believe they are the problem. If you were taught you are the problem depending on the nature of the fault, superficial, material, or moral, the individual is valued proportionally. This is not to make parents less than who they know they are, but to say we are not lacking in good parenting and leadership would be living in that alternate universe we mentioned above.

So we are in need of help in these areas, and in some cases because of our circumstances, we are left helpless. Because this is how we as a society and a culture have evolved, the children of this generation will walk in what we as parents have lead them to believe is true. *When who we are told we are leads us to believe less about what we can accept about ourselves, life becomes difficult.*

Maybe then you can understand why a teen mom would be able to justify leaving her baby at a doorstep somewhere or worse. I know this is a quantum leap for some, but remember in the world of reality that the truth is your friend.

So to ask who's at fault and who's to blame, I would say I'm sure there is enough blame to go around. But what I believe about the truth is it's timeless and can at this very moment be a saving help for someone in any given situation. But the effect that truth has on the human spirit is what we need to focus on.

Why do people who go through terrible circumstances in life become famous leaders and great parents, yet others fall prey to the convictions and guilt placed on them either through a mistake or faults or people in their lives? Because without a greater good to bow to, the moral equivalent of our faults will only produce bondage and hopelessness.

And the pursuit of happiness becomes nothing but a fairy tale. The lie that this is the way things are and they will never change has robbed us of these certain inalienable rights we are born with. The American dream is no longer a reality. In this dog-eat-dog world where only the good die young and no good deed should go unpunished, hopelessness has robbed and devalued our society of its most valuable resource—our young.

Guilt

Guilt is the prison where the hopeless will serve their sentence. When innocence is lost, the key to unlocking that cage is nowhere to be found. In the human spirit, hope springs eternal, but without hope, the loss of innocence, and enough guilt, this for some could be a life sentence, and for some, it truly is. The hope to set the prisoner free is truth. Without truth, reconciliation will be impossible. We as human beings are not able to ignore feelings of guilt. We either let the truth be known and get on the road to recovery, or we do as some psychiatrists say to do just ignore it or medicate it. Neither of which have worked with any real results. When I say real results, I am referring to restoring innocence. Because until innocence can be restored, guilt will have its way. And by the research we covered, one would conclude by their own results that the psychological approach is failing.

To be in bondage to our mistakes, faults, shortcomings, regrets, or just missing the mark is the human condition, and without bringing blame into the equation, I will call it, yes, sin. The biblical context of sin is just missing the mark without blame as the ultimate reason because we all fall short.

If we need a reason or an excuse for some of our behavior at times because it becomes unbearable, casting blame can be the drug of choice to ease the pain. But if and when there is no excuse and you believe you are the problem, guilt is where you will live out your sentence, and blame is the taskmaster. I think the problem today is that we are in such bondage to sin (oh, I mean not being perfect or just missing the mark). Adding blame, shame, and regret to the mix makes our burden of guilt so unbearable that we imprison ourselves to a life sentence of helplessness.

We were never made to carry the weight of guilt that we place on ourselves or by others due to poor choices or mistakes. But because our conscience does not live up to our integrity or our expectations of ourselves, we take responsibility and carry the guilt.

We may believe this is a just penalty we deserve and can be a lifetime sentence. The problem is this has no redeeming qualities, and we end up again hopeless.

So where is the peace and love we were promised in the sixties? What happened to live-and-let-live approach to life that was supposed to change the world and all of the humanistic philosophies of the eighties, nineties, and now?

Some of the greatest social and philosophical minds on human behavior and social engineering are not succeeding in making the world a better place, at least not the world I'm living in.

To me, peace is a place where the mind is satisfied, the will is surrendered, and our emotions at rest.

Unfortunately, this condition is mostly unattainable because we have lost our innocence.

Guilt, blame, shame, regret, excuse, and helplessness are insurmountable against the attempts to regain peace. In our world today, peace has become a conditioned and temporary oasis at best, a world where we are in bondage to ourselves.

And that's the truth. Ask any parent how they would begin to instill hope and peace into a child without deviating from the truth? Because of what our children are taught, that task is no easy lesson.

Guilt is the opposite of innocence, and I am not trying to say we by our nature possess innocence. But if we are not guilty of some accusations brought against us, well, then we owe it to ourselves to get some resolution. Now some people are better at this than others. But I also know that this fight can at times become exhausting. I guess that's why we need Superman as an example who always won in the fight for truth, justice, and the American way. We were never made to fight this fight alone and is unattainable without some form of reconciliation. If we believe that the truth is more powerful than a lie and forgiveness is greater than sin or missing the mark, that justification is greater than what we blame ourselves for, then we can have hope. If what we bring is truth in our defense as a sacrifice for innocence then because truth is benign, this law applies, "*If the innocence of the sacrifice is greater than the guilt of the offense*, then guilt has no place, and redemption is possible." So where is innocence found?

Guilt has no past, is in the present tense, dictates your future, affects everyone you are in relationship with, limits your potential, will paralyze your intentions, hampers your progress, robs your strength, will compromise your purpose, stunts you ambitions, and makes you blind to the truth. Now that is the best definition of incarceration I have ever heard—in prison to your past with no hope for the future.

Shame

If guilt is not enough to steal our identity, then shame is the evidence we use to believe guilt is a just sentence. And if without hope we imprison ourselves, then shame determines the length of the sentence. As long as shame is not dealt with, it will slam the door on our innocence and will lead to a helpless state of mind where hopelessness and depression are just a shot away.

Shame is powerful; it will bring you to your knees, and it doesn't matter how egregious the offense is. What matters is how it affects your conscience or your spirit. If you are gifted and talented, your gifts and talents are ingrained in your character. They are the certain unalienable rights mentioned in our constitution that our Creator has endowed us with.

The value you find in yourself in having these gifts can be scarred and damaged by shame. Shame is a by-product of wrongdoing, and our spirit or our conscience bears witness to the wrong done. People of good character will be compelled to seek out the truth or suffer the consequences. But if their character is not integrated, they are the ones who suffer the most for their shortcomings.

Our character or temperament, if you will, is how we deal with life as a whole. It's what makes us tick and can be shaped by our conscience. *Integrity is a moral standard by which we set the bar, and our significance is valued on how well we live up to our integrity.*

Ultimately we want to be the person we have defined, and the goal is to integrate our character and our integrity and be who we have set out to be. In his book *Integrity*, Dr. Henry Cloud contributes both material, social, and personal fulfillment to an integrated character.

But when we are damaged either by guilt, shame, or blame, the only antidote is truth. If what you believe in is not the truth, then the endless cycle of a baseless mind-set haunts our conscience or our spirit man and is suppressed and/or medicated. The damage that is incurred is dependent on the level of giftedness we possess, and obviously, the more value lost, the greater the regret. Well, you get the message.

It should be important to know that what you believe is the truth. For it's the truth that will set you free. To ignore this is the first step to helplessness that ends in an endless cycle that uses more emotional energy than one is made to handle, unless they are ignored, suppressed, or medicated.

It should be no wonder then why these statistics are overwhelming and how they play into the hands of reality. You will reap what you sow, but the seeds of despair we are planting come at the cost of a human life, and this is the bare truth. In a culture with a mind-set of hopelessness, survival has diminished substantially. That's just a way of saying we believe we are worthless.

As I am writing this, my sons told me that one of their high-school friend has passed away at thirty-six, the owner of a successful snowboard-accessory company. What could possibly be the reason he chose to consume enough alcohol to make life short? Apparently his wife cheated on him and left, and he never recovered. Unfortunately, this scenario has been the cause of a multitude of suicides. A broken heart is one of the hardest lessons in life to go through.

Love is a give and take, but it's my belief that if you give too much to the wrong person at the wrong time, the effects could last a lifetime and could inhibit your ability to trust enough to have a healthy relationship in the future. There are parts of us that are sacred, and I'm not sure we fully grasp the gravity of that statement. If you give the sacred to the unworthy, you will pay the consequences. And some of you have paid dearly. I would venture to say that most of us, if not all of us, can share in being mentally and emotionally bankrupt due to throwing some pearls before swine. But how we recover and who we become because of these affairs will determine our ability to go into any future relationships unscarred and most importantly without bringing any attitude or our own insignificance into the relationship. You can't give away what you don't possess, so if you have nothing good to give to a relationship, you're already off to a bad start. To be hurt by the people we love can be the greatest contributor to hopelessness. But hopefully you will read this book before it's too late, and you can redeem the relationship you are now in.

We are led to believe that the shame, blame, mistakes, and faults are part of the human experience, and we are doomed to live out that sentence in our everyday lives. We are hopeless. Although we may not want to confront our human condition, the underlying truth is its effects are a price too heavy for some of us to carry. And relief is not spelled Rolaids, although heartburn is surely not off the list of side effects due to this condition.

The inability to continue to bear the burdens of life is a common problem. The stress that life brings is played out in our neighborhoods across the nation and around the world.

We are looking for peace, and it seems that the best we can do is create new laws that only tax the real problem. The cry of the human heart for the peace we can't attain will continue because we don't know where to get it.

It is as this unknown poet says, "As a rule man's a fool when it's hot he wants it cool; when it's cool he wants it hot, always wanting what is not." Yet I am forced to ask the question why.

Why are we never satisfied or content? Can hope and innocence be restored, and can the truth really set us free? Not when shame is in the game.

Fear

One of the best acrostics I have heard to describe fear is *False Evidence Appearing Real.* The claim that the highest percentage of the fears we deal with is baseless, I think, is an understatement. Fear coupled with false accusations are crippling. False accusations are the number one cause of fear. I can't begin to tell you the numerous cases of false accusation that led to the accused being found guilty.

Our prisons are full of innocent people who are a by-product of fear-based false accusations, and DNA has become the truth serum in more and more cases of falsely accused individuals who have spent most of their lives in prison for a crime they did not commit.

But the truth is, where the insignificance of life is a standard by which we judge the innocent, we have retarded the process. When the accusations bring more of a burden on truth before due process, fear will unlock the door to incrimination. Fear, I believe, has led to the many false confessions that have been made, and the hopelessness of our human condition is what we submit as proof before the truth is revealed. The number of suicides due to false accusations are too many to mention.

This to me is a stark reminder of the overwhelming responsibility of the judges and justices of our land. We can only hope that they can fulfill their most noble duty to bring *liberty and justice for all.*

So if the doubts and fears we are led to believe are allowed to dictate the course of our lives, where is the truth and the justice in that? It has given way to hopelessness. But we should never fear the truth. Perfect love founded on the truth casts out fear.

Denial

Coping is a treadmill that keeps us keeping on. It's the "hang in there" motto adopted by most of us law-abiding moral citizens who just want to live out our lives in peace. But the truth is, in the real world where time and change are inevitable, they are ignored at your own risk.

Time brings change; circumstance demands action, and we deal with circumstance the same as before. We ignore it and allow it to overtake us. Been there, done that.

To allow life to work itself out only works if you live alone on a deserted island somewhere between a blissful thought and the perfect life. But no, it's not that easy; we are compelled to get on that treadmill and walk out our life one day or one hour or one minute at a time depending on whether you are in a coping or crisis mode. For the most part, coping is a good mechanism.

The truth is, if coping brings comfort, it can lead to denial. To ignore a fact is not bliss. One of the biggest lies I remember growing up was "what you don't know can't hurt you." Wow, just listen to that statement. "Or ignorance is bliss." Try that as a plea in a court of law. No, what you don't know can destroy you. One of my favorite Bible verses is "My people are destroyed from lack of knowledge" (Hosea 4:6, NIV). And like all of the lessons we can learn from the Bible, this still holds true today. Let me say, even more today. It is one of those transcendent things we mentioned above. Coping is a great way to deal with an issue with less stress, but that should only be till the real answers come. I am in no way foreign to the pain and frustration of life, and patience is not my virtue. Just ask my wife. Maybe you better not; she can write a sequel to this book.

The lessons we learn as we cope with the things we don't have answers to are what makes us who we are. *However, we can't allow coping to replace hope.* It becomes a dead work. To adopt a coping mentality can get very comfortable. Nero played the fiddle while Rome burned.

And so a coping mentally can bring relief, but let's not ignore the heart of the matter. Just like a heart surgeon cannot just remove a heart and expect their patient to survive, we can't just eliminate the inevitable by ignoring it. If you ignore the truth and you become ignorant to the facts, truth is transcendent; it can't change. And ignoring it has consequences.

When we ignore the truth, time and circumstance will not work to your favor, and the end result is the blame being placed on someone or something that's called *denial*. Ignorance and denial can become bedfellows, especially if you have adopted a hopeless mind-set. And not only is it easy and painless; it has become a way of life for an ever-growing part of society.

Family problems, out-of-control children, all types of abuse, and divorce are the by-products of not dealing with the reality of life. To ignore the truth is not an option. The inevitable circumstances of life will overtake you, and you will have to gain your strength from another trivial pursuit, leaving you and everyone you are in relationship with on your island desolate.

I am always amazed at how creative we become in justifying our purpose for not dealing with an issue. I could write a book on the reasons why we don't go to church, and it would probably be a best seller. What the heck, I'll never know when I might need one myself.

To be lost and knowing you're lost can be frustrating and downright scary at times. But to be lost and not know leaves us in a far greater place of vulnerability and danger; to believe a lie has consequences and to not know what the truth is, is really the same thing, but the consequences do not become any less, and they don't simply vanish through not knowing what the truth is. So here is why "my people are destroyed for lack of knowledge" (Hosea 4:6, NIV).

The determining factor between believing and knowing is locked up in the conscience of every human being. So you may ask, how will I know? When you weigh the facts against the truth, you will by your convictions know what direction to go in. Just don't fool yourself into thinking that no action is needed or the truth doesn't apply to your situation. If you ask, what is truth? Pilate who crucified Jesus and every judge needs to find the answer to that question. But in judging ourselves, the jury better not be out. The alternative is denial.

If for you coping has given way to denial, I hope these words will allow you to take inventory and make an assessment of the truth about your situation. And I will let you in on a secret. When you ignore the truth for any amount of time, you become foolish.

And I learned that when I am foolish, the only person I'm fooling is myself, and there are not two people involved. There is only one fool making those decisions. Believing we are okay when we are not will never allow us to rest because of the hopelessness this produces. One of our churches' core values is "It's okay not to be okay. But it's not okay to stay that way."

And let me add, "Or you will be doomed to repeat the same faults and mistakes," and in the end, you will only find insignificance, foolishness, and hopelessness.

Chapter 2
We Can't Keep Doing This

Doing the same thing over again and expecting a different result has been called insanity. If we take an honest look at our lives, we would all agree that there are things we would never attempt again. And sociologically speaking, you would think mankind would have by now found a place in history that we could say of some things we will never let that happen again. I think of Adolf Hitler and the holocaust, of Stalin, Mao Zedong, Kim Jung-il, Pol Pot, Bashar al-Assad, just to name a few. These monsters are what most of us would call evil. And most of us would say we shall never again allow these events to tarnish human history.

I say most of us because the more I try to keep up with the modern worldviews, I realize there are some among us who would defend these atrocious acts and chock them up to a bad mix of atoms and molecules. Now before you say I'm exaggerating, I must tell you I am not.

When a leading atheist was asked, "If we do not acknowledge some external standard for morality, what is to prevent us from saying Muslim extremist aren't right since the atheistic view is we are really at the mercy of our DNA and therefore no guilt or wrongdoing can actually be assessed to these acts?" Richard Dawkins has been quoted as saying, "Well, what's to prevent us from saying that Hitler wasn't right?" He called it a difficult question. Listen to that, a difficult question. Is it just me, or are we losing all logic? Is there some type of foolish thinking when it comes to morals? To have this worldview of moral relativism is, as you can see, a dangerous direction to be headed. Yet the argument rages on and has taken over the prevailing view or the thinking of most of what is being taught in our colleges today. Now I'm not saying that our colleges are condoning these atrocities, but moral relativism is becoming the norm, adopting a live-and-let-live attitude when it comes to right and wrong. To be wrong and to be convinced that somehow by believing it will change its outcome or the effect to our folly is ignorance, or would some agree with me if I said insanity?

The transcendent things in life can never change. They can be ignored, but it's at our own peril, and unfortunately a vast majority of our youth are headed in that direction. As I have just returned from vacation in two short weeks, there has been two more cases of overdose in our town. And this week I had met a man at work whose twenty-one-year-old son died from an overdose. As I sat in a meeting, we have to pray for young-adult children; one of our friends' son is a police officer in our town, and she mentioned in the short time he has been on the force that he has had to cut down eleven hangings by suicide.

What is generating all the hopelessness and desperation that leads an individual to choose to bury their future in a drug-infested culture that breeds death?

Can the questions that are at the heart of where life is headed today weigh so heavy on the human conscience that a life-or-death choice is demanded? The problem is the choice that these individuals are being left with does not satisfy the longing in the human spirit. I watched a Jewish historian give a speech on a college campus recently on the Jewish holocaust, and he had mentioned that his views could be read in the pamphlets he had handed out. At the end of his talk, he had a question-and-answer session. A young Muslim woman came to the mic and asked why the Muslim faith was not given any attention in his pamphlet. He explained he had, but she wanted to make a point that he was not fair in his assessment of how the Muslims were portrayed. When he realized she had an agenda because of a symbol she wore, he asked if she agreed with the beliefs of Hezbollah. She said that because she would be incriminated if she made her beliefs known, she couldn't answer the question. Then he asked whether she could agree with a quote from a prominent Hezbollah leader who said, "He wished that all the Jews would congregate at one time in Jerusalem so it would be easier to annihilate them." He asked, "Agree or disagree?" Without hesitation, she said agree. Someone help me process this. This is a twenty-plus-year-old college student.

A well-known Christian apologist visited some mainstream college campuses. The response from students to some of his questions was a litmus test of how they view life as a whole. One question was, "If your neighbor and a dog were drowning in a lake after falling through the ice and you could only save one, who would that be?" If I told you that without hesitation some chose the dog, would that surprise you? If you said yes, then read on. If you say no, then you share my concern as to why this book is being written. Our college campuses are breeding grounds for leftist professors who are not tolerant for any type of religious creationistic worldview, and God help you if you happen to have a Christian or a Jewish worldview or any belief in intelligent design.

I think of two recent movie releases, *God's Not Dead 2* and Ben Stein's

Expelled: No Intelligence Allowed. In both cases, the attack from the left was appalling. In the movie *Expelled: No Intelligence Allowed,* Ben Stein goes on a fact-finding mission to uncover the bias against intelligent-design proponents. Now the controversy was over an article by Dr. Steven Meyer, the author of *Signature in the Cell: DNA and the Evidence for Intelligent Design.* His article was reviewed by his peers and was printed in a prominent scientific magazine. When he received some good reviews by a Dr. von Stromberg who was on the scientific team for the Smithsonian, Dr. Stromberg was fired for merely considering that the intelligent-design theory had some validity and was a creditable avenue of thought.

What was striking to me was the response of his peers who did not agree with this theory. They were not at all tolerant and were quick to terminate Dr. von Stromberg.

In the movie *Expelled: No Intelligence Allowed,* Ben Stein shows how numerous examples were made of the so-called opponents of Darwinian evolution.

Now I'm not a scientist and have not studied the sciences or DNA or molecular design. But it's common sense to me that if a study of any kind has shown merit, it should be pursued, especially in the science community. Think of where we would be if the scientists researching a cure for cancer had this kind of bias.

Listen to Dr. Fred Hoyle, an English astronomer and cosmologist scientist and mathematician, who said, "The likelihood of the formation of life from inanimate matter is 1 to the number 40,000." He also said, "The chance that higher life forms might have emerged through the evolutionary process is comparable to a tornado sweeping through a junk yard and assembling a 747." And he ended by saying, "Yet I refuse to believe in a God who created the universe." What prevents him from believing in a Creator?

Truth or Consequences

In a conference recently, the top atheists met to discuss the intelligent-design theory and its effects on atheism.

Because of the insurmountable evidence of the intellectual structure of DNA, in opposition they now claim we as humans are a product of an alien seedpod. And matter as we know it, we came into being on the back of crystals. It's anything but God. And we are scolded when we refuse to accept their theories. There is a danger to this set of beliefs. Remember, to believe in a false theory does not make it true. The world is not flat. And the emperor had no clothes. But when you blatantly deny the facts in the face of the plain truth, I have to call it a lie. But who determines when denial becomes a lie? Is it a lie or rebellion? Call it what you want, but when an excuse is made for not acknowledging plain facts that I will call truth, we have a problem. Are plain facts truth, or do we excuse ourselves because we do not agree? Now I do respect the opinions of others, and America is the land of the free, but if freedom and truth do not fit in the same box and the two get separated until they are reconciled, they will devalue each other until the choices that are left are meaningless and futile. Think about it, if you refuse to accept the fact that the world is round and you set out to find the edge of the world because the map you're using is flat, you will be on an endless journey to nowhere. And when reality and circumstance collide or when that ship you're on runs out of fuel, you will be faced with the truth. *To deny the truth can lead to self-deprivation.* When we deny the truth, we are fooling ourselves. And there are not two people making the decisions. There is only one fool. In the battle for truth, justice, and the American way, truth always wins; pride always loses no matter what we think!

Nevertheless, it seems there is a campaign on the left to keep this intelligent-design theory out of any mainstream science curriculum.

They have targeted any institution that would teach this or any design theory from grade school and up. In Pennsylvania, the ACLU fought successfully against the creation theory being taught as an alternative worldview.

I am not trying to make a case for any worldview because I believe the facts should speak for themselves and because I believe that people are very capable of forming their own opinion.

But there is a danger in this kind of morally relative baseless thinking that can't be overlooked. If your morals are relative to your circumstances and your DNA and your existence on earth is tied to a baseless concept of an animalistic instinct, then life becomes a futile attempt at a useless existence, especially to those less fortunate or to those with strong convictions, and that unfortunately includes the gifted and talented.

That leaves us at the mercy of chance and circumstance. I don't think I am alone in saying that I refuse to sit by while the lives of people, young and old, are being tarnished by an unfounded set of beliefs.

The Real Problem

The real problem is every human being is created with the innate sense to decipher right from wrong. If not, this world would be a dangerous and corrupt place. And at the root of the problem is an unraveling of the human spirit, *the conscience with which we determine right or wrong.* At what point, if ever, do things that violate our conscience become bad? And who sets the moral standard? If doing things that violate our conscience become accepted, there is no self-worth in doing good. Self-worth is found when we are able to reproduce in others the will to depend on their gifts and talents that make a change in themselves and the people in their lives. It's parenting 101. However, worthlessness is a breeding ground for social decadence. If you are led to believe that you have no self-worth, and that's the road that most of today's youth are on, the outcome is played out in real life, whether we want it to happen or not. Whatever you believe about yourself becomes a self-proclaimed prophecy. There are consequences to believing something that is not true when you base your convictions on it. Thoughts are canisters for emotions and actions. To act on an untruth has consequences. First, you are doomed to repeat the past with a false premise, and second, the loss of worth and the significance we lose can cause numerous problems from worthlessness to alcohol and drug abuse to acting out of frustration and is a by-product of not being able to rationalize our own view to a standard of truth that would bring a sense of self-acceptance critical for our well-being both mentally and emotionally.

To be able to stand on the truth shifts the burden of proof away from us and allows for the tranquility in our souls—*our mind, will, and emotions*— we so critically need to find purpose and significance. Significance can only happen if our convictions on what we believe can rest on the truth, and our conscience and our will are at rest. Self-acceptance is the remedy for confusion and doubt and is the first step to redeeming the human spirit. But it must be founded on truth. Anybody with me?

The problem is when we try to accept or validate a wrong mind-set or behavior, we do more damage than good, and that leads to bondage. Bondage only occurs when what we believe is not true, and the burden of proof falls on us personally. We are bound by our convictions, and when our awareness of what is right is not true, our conscience is violated; then we are forced to defend our beliefs in spite of the facts.

The amount of emotional breakdowns played out in everyday life is staggering. Whether at home, work, on the road, on line at the grocery store, in politics, and even in our churches, we can't ignore the uneasiness of life we all experience today. But when what we believe in is true, the burden of proof stands on its own merit.

But why has life become so desperate? Could it be that the uneasiness about who we are, what our purpose is here on earth, and that the effects of believing in the baseless concept of the futility of life with no purpose has undermined the hope that springs eternal in the human spirit?

This worthlessness is a product of a worldview that has become the basis of what we have allowed ourselves to believe. Yet we allow ourselves to devalue life by being led to believe less than the truth about ourselves and life in general. Dr. Martin Luther King said, "A man that has not found something worth dying for is not fit to live." But that *something* must bear witness to our conscience and give the believer a purpose of limitless value, something beyond the limits of what we value so as to increase our self-worth. Remember, every human being needs to be accepted loved and approved, and the reality is, truth is the best medicine for people who lack these basic needs.

For the human spirit to be set free to allow that person to grow to their full potential, we cannot force them to believe in anything but the facts. However, this has to be a conscious, willful decision to allow the truth to be our schoolmaster so when we are judged on our value, it will prove to the individual that their commitment is not in vain. When you have come to terms with the truth, your next step is maturity. But it must be obvious by now that we can't keep doing the same things.

Our conscience is a delicate part of our psyche. If it is violated from any outside source, our principles are called into question, and a decision is demanded in order to support our convictions. If it is violated from within, our moral structure is challenged, and we are compelled to make changes that support our principles. But if our conscience is violated from these outside sources that are based on principles that are portrayed as truth and are not, we will make changes and decisions that will undermine our significance. The emotional cost of doing business in the area of truth can either help or hurt us because truth is transcendent. *Truth or consequences.* Without the lighthouse of truth, our consciences are doomed to be broken on the rocks of our convictions. To be ignorant or to ignore the truth is why justice is blind but not to consequences. To lead someone to believe anything but the truth when you are an authoritarian in any area is socially unjust.

So I'll say it again, we can't keep doing this. If any of this makes sense to you, then you are on the way to understanding the purpose of this book. The truth is what will redeem the human spirit.

To believe in a life filled with purpose or as Pastor Rick Warren puts it, *a purpose-driven life*, has an altogether different meaning compared to some prominent worldviews. But the path to get there has to start with something worth perusing. And I'm not sure we are going in the right direction.

To discover your purpose in furthering a cause for a greater good versus someone else's cause is where I think the difference is. The latter lacks personal significance.

But to promote a theory based on someone's opinion or agenda and to ignore the factual evidence sounds to me like fascism and goes against our First Amendment rights.

Believe It or Not

In light of the most recent findings, Darwin's theory of evolution is proving to be just that, a theory. But in the light of today's social agenda, there is no room for any truth or facts that will be considered contrary to his theory. Most of us would consider this to be disingenuous at the least and unacceptable for many.

But the story doesn't end here. Eugenie Scott, an American physical anthropologist, is working to prevent creationism from being taught in public schools. Now if Darwinian evolution is a proven fact, then I say, "Let's move on." But the fact of the matter is, Darwin himself said of his theory that it still had a burden of proof that he believed would be proven after further research and time. But as time and research have proven, there are things so complex about life that the scientific studies of today's research proves the Darwinian theory is not the smoking gun we are led to believe it is. So let's let people as individuals hear the truth and decide for themselves if we are allowed to.

Now I don't know about you, but the end of that sentence "if we are allowed to" should not be there, but the truth is we are being force-fed a theory that is losing validity in the science community. No one should ever be allowed to decide what the belief of someone else should be.

And the battle for the minds of our youth and the fate of who we are as a nation rages on to the detriment of the moral fabric of our society. The fact of the matter is, if you control the learning institutions, you control the society.

The battle for the minds of our youth is not taken lightly with the opponents of any opposing worldview that is now being taught.

Any opposing view is viciously attacked both legally and at the grassroots level before it is allowed to stand on its own merits.

We can't keep doing this, believing and teaching a theory and force-feeding it to our society as truth. We do this to the determent of our creditability as freethinkers and the integrity of our cause as being endowed by our Creator with certain inalienable rights.

However, in the light of our present circumstances and where we are in our views today, any change has to start at the individual level.

So I think there are bigger questions we should be asking ourselves like when in his *evolution*, did man trust himself to make decisions on what is morally right, and against what standard can he evaluate his claims? If we are to redeem the human spirit from the bondage of a social agenda, we need to ask some moral questions. These decisions can only be formed by a conscientious decision made by individual convictions.

So at what point did he, man, become human making decisions based on a moral conscience? And in light of the fact that animals are not capable of making moral decisions but are governed by stimulated behavior, their instincts, survival of the fittest, and sex by any stimulation, what then separates us from the animal kingdom? Or are we being influenced by the underlying view to believe we are part of an animalistic progression of the evolutionary process? No, I believe that free will and the freedom to choose for ourselves by our own moral convictions is the difference between a civilized person and an animal. To believe the latter is self-destructive to our own worth and self-significance and is a malice to society. There should be a great deal of concern on the part of any parent who is trying to raise a child with a wholesome view to life that will build self-reliance and allow them to make decisions based on true facts and not on the opinion of others. I was listening to a radio commentator who was commenting on a study on the neurons in the brains of humans and animals. The study showed that humans have an extra layer of neurons that promote us to ask questions. No wonder dogs behave so well; they don't ask questions.

There is a war for the souls of our youth, but it is obvious to me that if we continue on the same course, we will reap the fruits of doing the same thing. There is a Bible verse that says, "Because sentence against an evil work is not executed speedily, therefore the heart of the sons of men is fully set in them to do evil" (Ecclesiastes 8:11, AKJV). And because we as parents have not dealt with sin decisively, the children will now pay the price. Hard words to hear.

The current worldview acts as an opiate to our human frailty and is condescending to the freedom of the human spirit *that certain inalienable right* we as Americans have fought for since our forefathers gave us these precepts as the foundation of this great land we call America, founded on the *proposition that all men are created equal*—equal to think and believe the truth, not to be forced into a theory that stands in the way of the freethinking we were endowed with.

Yet as we are seeing, there is a mind-set or a worldview that this America is somehow responsible for the trouble the world sees itself in now, and we need to repent and humble ourselves before the nations and take responsibility for our shortcomings. Humility is power under control, not conceding the truth to benefit the opinion of a particular group of people.

The latter is folly. And to fail to transcend to the greater good will only lead to more chaos because like a lighthouse not heeding its warnings, we are doomed to crash into the rocks and break into pieces.

And in my opinion, not only is this where we are headed as a society today, but the fruits of the hope and the dreams we as people harbor in our hearts is being denied, and a culture of death born out of desperation has taken their place.

Science will never be able to explain away the existence of the human conscience.

Then by our freedom of choice, are we not redeemed to be free to choose between right and wrong? That is our soul's right, and no one should be allowed to make those decisions for us. So what's the big fuss over?

Well, for years we are taught the theory of evolution as fact. Now microevolution is the process of change within its own kind and is easily acceptable and can be observed over time.

The observation over time of any given study is by definition the basis of the science we all are familiar with. And within its kind is simply cats becoming lions and dogs both big and small evolving into wolves, etc.

But macroevolution is the belief (I say belief because there was no one here millions of years ago to observe these changes, and they are purely made by believing in how things changed) that fish evolved into man without any observable evidence. Without observation over time, macroevolution is a theory based on blind faith. To believe in something you have no solid evidence for is a faith-based belief system, but to promote it as truth and defend it is deception.

As we have had advances in science and the study of DNA, we are now faced with the truth that macroevolution, a belief in a theory of unobservable evidence, is just what it claims to be, a theory. And as we advance in our understanding of the cell and the complexity of even the most simple protein, we have overwhelming evidence to support an intelligent-design theory.

Then why would any opposition to the theory of evolution be so hostile to viable intelligent studies and advances that may have another view or theory other than their own? Many world-renowned scientists are on the record as saying it is taboo to hold to any view opposed to Darwinian evolution.

And to voice any view that even mentions *intelligent design* is a sure way to have your resignation requested. Yet the more we look at the complexity of the cell, DNA, and even our environment, we are drawn into the direction of some intellect or pattern of design codes found in our DNA and the perfect order of the universe.

For instance, the designs found in DNA are so complex that most scientists are amazed at not only the complexity but the system and structure of how it all fits together.

Now words like *system* and *structure* may not be acceptable in the world of mainstream evolutionary science. *And not all scientists are evolutionists.* But that does not erase the facts.

The DNA codes reveal the complexity of the cell that had Darwin had the technology of today, his theory would not have been his conclusion. He said that time and study, *observance of change over time*, real science is what was needed to prove his theory. But believing him to be a true scientist basing his conclusions on the facts and he being able to observe the complexity of the cell as the research today shows has implications that are astounding that I think would surely affect his findings.

I've heard that the coded DNA cell explained as a scrabble game. The coded DNA message is like having a triple word score. For you scrabble players, that speaks volumes.

But there is an underlying problem with why I believe we cannot continue doing the same thing over again. Charles Darwin published *The Descent of Man, and Selection in Relationship to Sex* which was applied to the origin of the species and became controversial. It basically made reference to the fact that less fortunate, the mentally ill, or people born with any maladies or birth defect should or could be socially engineered out of existence either by natural selection or by choice. Many chose to play God and help this change take place for the betterment of the society. Mandatory sterilization of thousands in Germany became part of this effort.

Those following this theory and putting it to practice committed well-documented atrocities that led to some of the darkest times of science research.

There was a belief that we could engineer sickness, physical or mental, out of society by sterilizing any people that had a history of these maladies in their family history. In 1833, British explorer and natural scientist Frances Galton, influenced by Darwin's theory of natural selection, advocated a system that would allow "the more suitable races or strains of blood a better chance to prevail speedily over the less suitable," therefore creating a master race.

The eugenics movement began in the United States in the late nineteenth century and focused on effort to stop the transmission of negative or undesirable traits from generation to generation. In response to these ideas, some US leaders, private citizens, and corporations started funding eugenic studies that lead to the 1911 establishment of the Eugenics Records Office (ERO) in Cold Spring Harbor, New York.

This movement was spearheaded by Margret Sanger, the founder of Planned Parenthood. The ERO spent time tracking family histories and concluded that people deemed to be unfit more often came from families that were poor, low in the social standing, migrant, and/or minority. Stricter immigration rules were enacted, but the most ominous resolution was a plan to sterilize *unfit* individuals to prevent them from passing on their negative traits. A total of thirty-three states had sterilization programs in place. While initially targeting the mentally ill, it later included alcoholism, criminality, chronic poverty, blindness, deafness, feeblemindedness, and promiscuity. It was not uncommon for African American women to be sterilized during other medical procedures without consent.

I hope there are some black people reading this book because I have lost respect for anyone who believes that someone's intellect has anything to do with race or skin color.

At this point, let me say I would definitely give anyone who claims to be an evolutionist the benefit of the doubt on this. But please let me explain why I take that approach.

Social Darwinism was a popular theory in the late nineteenth century that said that life for humans in society was ruled by the survival of the fittest, which helped advance eugenics. Margret Sanger, the founder of Planned Parenthood, was a famed proponent of eugenics and had encouraged the location of Planned Parenthood clinics be located in black neighborhoods. I guess the thought was that blacks were not able to contribute to society on a ratio of what they were taking from society. Anyone feeling queasy yet?

The sick or feebleminded were atrociously exterminated in Germany. The premise was that these misfits are consuming good food and water to no good end.

This is well documented, and I found it very disturbing to find that some of these experiments were even practiced in the United States as we saw above.

Our own government was involved in the UNFPA, the United Nations Fund for Population Activities, but in 2017, we withdrew funding. We should applaud the decisions of our leaders who make decisions on facts, not on our status or worldview.

But the overall mind-set that life is somehow valued on the opinion of science and has a higher or lower value based on location, behavior, maladies, or the strength of someone's immune system undermines these certain inalienable rights our freedom is founded on.

Consider the following: Louis Braille was a blind organist. John Stanley was blind from childhood and Succeeded Handel as a director. Beethoven was tormented by deafness, and an autopsy showed he was born with a malformed inner ear.

If an expectant mom walked in to a clinic looking for counseling for reproduction and her family history was one of premature infant deaths due to chronic syphilis, she would most likely be counseled to consider terminating the pregnancy. That choice would have aborted Mozart as his mother had lost five out of seven children.

Yet today in our society, life is looked at as expendable. There are a few states today where they will pay 100 percent for an abortion up to nine months and now, as of late, after delivery. I need to stop for a moment. Please excuse me. Who does this? And then to treat a curable ailment is in some cases unaffordable.

Why have we allowed the devaluation of life to a point of despair that is played out in the lives of both young and old today? Then we ask why we are wrestling with what's right and wrong. Or are we competing with one another for the soul of America and for the redemption of the human spirit?

Everyone today from the high-school students to world leaders will agree that something has to and will change. And I will add that the feeling is that this change is imminent.

So my question is, does change occur from outside the human experience through circumstance beyond our control or by choices people make based on what they know and believe? I think we will all agree that we can change the outcome by our choices. Can we generate change, or are we foolish enough to choose chance over choice? The path we take in life will determine our destiny. And what we believe to be true will determine our direction. But we should never ignore the most valuable of these unalienable rights we are endowed with—the right to choose.

So the more we know about the truth, the better equipped we are to make the choices that can change not only our own destiny but change the course of history. I believe the responsibility is on this generation to make the right choices that will pave the way for a future and a hope that will lead to the reality that the human spirit is an unstoppable force for good that can and will change history. The choice is ours. But we can't keep doing the same thing.

Chapter 3
The Human Spirit and the Soul of a Nation

The soul of a nation is found in the convictions of its people.

We the people, the preamble to the constitution, is one of the building blocks of this great society.

And sadly, there is now more opposition to the tenets of what made this country great than ever before. It seems that the voice of a few has dominated the rights of the many with vain repetitious demands for their rights yet ignoring the values this nation was founded on.

Devaluation (the attempt to make something less than what it is by ignoring its validity to promote an opposition or an agenda) is never what brings about positive change. To sacrifice what is right, good, and wholesome for the sake of enacting someone's rights was never intended to be the purpose for which the constitution was written. However, we see time and again the attempt to usurp the authority of the bill of rights to change the direction of the nation.

One of the most disturbing things I have encountered this year was an article in *Teen Vogue* that gave in depth the proper way to have anal sex and make it an enjoyable experience. I don't know about you, but it disturbs me to have to write that, but the truth be known it's real. Is this the ideal for what we have allowed the freedom of speech that our constitution was founded on to represent? Or have we lost something?

The moral fabric of a society is what drives its values and promotes the ideals set forth by the convictions of its founders. However, freedom of expression and authority are not the same. Freedom of expression has no authority to change the truth or the facts about the foundational principles of our founders, yet time and again, we are led to believe that that is why the bill of rights was written.

To deny or ignore that the principles on which our founders set forth in the forming of America and to ignore the fact that they are Judeo-Christian values is a product of a progressive worldview prevalent in society today. To try to devalue or ignore the fact that this nation is founded on Judeo-Christian values is a deception that some in government have bought into. But the facts remain.

The effects of this worldview on society to me at its root is directly opposed to the Judeo-Christian principles our country is founded on. And some will go to great lengths to promote its anti-Judeo-Christian bias.

Consider the following, as taken from *America's God and Country: Encyclopedia of Quotations* by William J. Federer.

On July 9,1776, the Continental Congress authorized the Continental Army to provide chaplains for their troops.

General George Washington issued the order and appointed chaplains to every regiment. On that same day, he issued the general order to his troops stating, "The general hopes and trusts that every officer and man will endeavor to so live and act, as becomes a Christian soldier defending the dearest rights and the liberties of this country."

On October 11, 1798, President John Adams stated in his address to the military, "Our constitution was made only for a moral and religious people. It is wholly inadequate to the government of any other."

On July 4, 1821, John Quincy Adams stated, "From the day of the declaration...they the American people were bound by the laws of God, which they all, and by the laws of the Gospel, which they nearly all, acknowledged as the rules of conduct."

Warren G. Harding, the twenty-ninth president, in his inaugural address on March 4,1921, he recognized, "I have always believed in the inspiration of the Holy Scriptures, whereby they have become the expression to man of the word and the will of God."

Matthew Calbraith Perry, US Navy commander (1794–1858), stated, "I have just finished the bible; I make it a point to read it through every cruise. It is certainly a wonderful book, a most wonderful book. From boyhood I have taken a deep interest in Christianizing the heathen and imparting the knowledge of God's revealed truth everywhere."

Thomas Paine (1737–1803) was an American revolutionary author who said, "The cause of America is in great measure the cause of all mankind. Where, say some is the king of America? I tell you friend He regains above on his death bed his last words were 'I die in perfect composure and resignation to the will of my Creator God.'"

On June 1, 1774, as the colonies were seeking God's will as to whether they should break ties with England, George Washington made this entry in his diary, "Went to church and fasted all day."

Benjamin Harrison, the twenty-third president of the United States, in writing to his son Russell, "It is a great comfort to trust God, even if His providence is unfavorable. Prayer steadies one, when he is walking in slippery places, even if things asked for are not given." And the proof is insurmountable as to what the intent of our founders adopted to be the cornerstone of this great nation. *America's God and Country: Encyclopedia of Quotations*, a great read.

There are countless accounts of the dependency on the Bible as the foundation on which this republic stands one nation under God. It's plain to see our founders were intent on building on biblical, godly principles.

But if the constitution is an ever-changing document, as some say, then whatever those in power say should be added, eliminated, or changed is socially accepted.

I don't know about you, but this to me is one of the most detrimental concepts falsely attributed to the bill of rights. The building blocks of this society, the foundation that supports why we believe what we believe, are being removed one block at a time. And any good builder knows about the effects of a compromised foundation. To alter the basic structure in any way with a purpose and intent is what I would call social engineering.

Why God

Since the mention of God has such a personal effect on people, it's only fair that we consider these biblical principles and their effect on society. As much as can be said about biblical principles, it has been proven to be the most effective and beneficial form of government in the history of mankind for wherever the gospel is preached that society flourishes. I think that this is mainly because wherever sin is preached, the people are faced with their own lack of morality, but with Christianity, they are not left to their own devices to work out their deficiencies. The only antidote for a person's lack of ability to live up to the standard that their convictions place on them is to know the truth and to face reality. And these are the building blocks to salvation but not without God's help.

Without some form of outside intervention, this lack of moral correctness will limit their potential and over long periods of time will lead them to be a slave to their own weaknesses.

We all could use some correction, just ask my wife. That's one of those things that women and mature men can agree on.

The mention of God, however, affects people at such a personal level that it strikes a nerve and unwittingly demands a response. I believe that this involuntary response is a yearning that is within the heart of every human being to be set free from the things that hold them back from being who they want to be. It is a desperate cry from the depth of their soul to know and believe there is a God who will not reject, condemn, or betray them and will stand by them in their doubts, weaknesses, and convictions and who will answer questions like, "Who am I, and why am I here, or why am I me?" I challenge you to ask yourself why you are you. You're going to need help, I'm sure.

But in order to acknowledge a deity, there has to be a release of self-control. And to be able to release control of one's self is where I believe the problem lies. To acknowledge a deity and to learn to trust in the same defines the depth of character of that person. Let me explain. We all need acceptance. Without the affirmation of our peers and those in authority over us or those whose opinions we revere, we will be on an endless search for significance. The need to be affirmed and acknowledged is one of the basic essentials to personal growth. Without being acknowledged or affirmed, we run the risk of a number of social diseases.

I think of John Dillinger, public enemy number one, who at a young age while attending a church service with his grandmother answered an altar call. Then after being ignored for twenty minutes, he walked out vowing never to enter a church again. All he needed was to be acknowledged and accepted.

The personal effects of rejection are far more complex than we can imagine. Have you ever been at a place in life where being considered for a position (a job position, a chance to carry the ball, or an opportunity to minister at a church) the opportunity to be chosen for that position just thrilled your soul and at your core you knew it was for that purpose you were there? Although you may not have had the experience, you knew that you had the skills, and along with your convictions and potential, it was for such a time as this you were created.

And because of poor leadership or management and maybe political reasons, you were not chosen. And I'm sure that these decisions are not made without some consideration. However, an explanation by good leadership would be in order in these instances, but more times than not, that is not the case. From that point forward, the way you look at authority may never be the same. Please, for those in authority, I know these decisions may not be intentional. But I'm talking about leadership, not procedure. Please lend me your ear.

As some physiologists point out when a child is faced with the fallibility of their parent, it is then they realize they are alone in the world as an individual.

At that point, their character will lead them to act on their own, look for help elsewhere, or despair.

The response of the parent or a person in authority at times like these can be critical as to whether or not these individuals will be able yield to authority or view authority in a healthy way in the future.

The devaluation and loss of trust in situations like that can have a lasting effect on some people and especially on those who are sincere in their endeavors.

The Bible says, "Hope deferred makes a heart sick but when desire is fulfilled it is a tree of life" (Proverbs 13:12, Amplified Bible). And similarly today, there is no shortage of people sick at heart and hopeless. Read chapter one.

It's in times like these we need to learn to trust in a higher authority, a moral lawgiver who is not influenced by the flawed principles that we experience in life.

Now you can rationalize away the feelings of rejection we encounter in these situations, but truth be told, the more dedication and energy we put into our goals, goals driven out of core convictions, the deeper the rejection and the more it affects our attitude toward authority. After a few rounds of this, we develop a strategy to keep who we are and what we believe is safe and maybe start to doubt ourselves.

Unfortunately, the devaluation or the simple lack of interest in people is all too common in our churches today. I understand this is the devil's playground. But I am also aware of what the lack of experience in leadership has caused. (Please, I am not saying our churches don't have good leadership, and I apologize if I struck a nerve with any of you who are anointed and called by God to shepherd your people.) And if you have that calling, I'm sure I piqued your interest with what I said. So please let me say, "Thank you, pastors, for your concern. We need you now more than ever."

Yet this is not solely a church problem.

At this point, we either develop behaviors that numb or isolate us from the pain of rejection. We rebel, or we learn to depend on a higher authority or an outside source for significance. These alternate views and outside sources are endless. The depth of a person's character is determined by whether we learn to trust, retreat, doubt, or question authority. Bad character traits can be overcome, and good character can be formed by good leadership. But the depth of personal character will be found in how we as individuals respond to authority.

If we withdraw and ignore or deny we have personal deficiencies in how we rationalize our actions with our conscience when it comes to whether or not we yield to authority, we rebel, and we become a law unto ourselves. The product of this mistrust is due to the lack of trust in leadership and authority. Due to poor leadership, we become fearful of the truth, and we learn to defend the lie we believe. Why, because we can't trust in how others portray truth. When we are a law unto ourselves, we are easily deceived, and there is a divide. However, truth and deception can't live in the same heart. When desire becomes part of this equation, desire will always win because we see no reason to deprive ourselves of what we desire. We believe we are entitled to our desires because we have devalued life by the disappointments we have experienced as a lack of faith in people and life. The problem is we are what we believe about ourselves.

But if what we believe is not based on reality and truth, we are doomed to search for a place of self-respect and acceptance, a place of reliability where your purpose and self-worth are mutual to your cause (or your spiritual conviction, your human spirit).

I know this gets a little involved. Sorry, but I am compelled to write this book. The fact of the matter is we are easily led by the opinions of others. As a matter of fact, we trust in the knowledge of what they say we should believe or who we should be to the point that we become subservient to their ideals.

And when things get shaken, we are left to fight a war we know little about. And as I'm sure you can tell, the soul of our nation is in need of redemption that only truth can reach. I see protestors who are willing to go to jail for the cause at hand, but when you ask them why they believe in their cause, more than 75 percent say they don't know.

The Truth of the Matter

In order to maintain a self-image that has value and is acceptable to you as an individual, there are a few things that need to be considered.
1. Can what you value stand alone without a defense on your part?
2. Are what you value and what you believe one and the same?
3. Can what you value prove what you believe without excuse?
4. And are you willing to put all on the line and sacrifice for the sake of this cause?

When you evaluated your beliefs on the above, you can trust yourself to depend on your convictions for the simple reason that what you believe is true. And again I'll quote Dr. Martin Luther King, "A man that has not found something worth dying for is not ready for life."

However, most of what we believe is founded on the opinion of others. We as individuals have lost our sense of significance. Our worth is no longer determined by what we as individuals believe but in a false hope founded on social status, not on our own convictions but on a false narrative that promises what it can't deliver. It's no wonder both young and old are in despair.

The human spirit that God consciousness part of who we are and the moral code we use that determines what is right or wrong is dying to self-gratification, a problem that if not remedied will cause the deprivation we see today to multiply.

The self, the ego, fed with false hope or on unfounded principles will only lead to false belief; false beliefs deprived of the truth leads to despair, and if not redeemed, it will be the beginning of the end of a society. Our society has never been so desperate for truth as we are today. Look at the youth and teen overdose and suicide rate. What's alarming is the stats in chapter one. These stats are based on the age of ten to seventy years of age.

Or just read your history books to see where we are headed. It's true that history repeats itself. King Solomon was right; there is nothing new under the sun.

To know the truth about something and to know something is true are two different things. The first is to have knowledge of the truth. The second is personal. I think a personal encounter with truth is where we need to start.

But to just say it's not your responsibility, wash your hands, and let the crowd make their own decisions never absolves you of the consequences. Remember, Pilate did the same thing and is one of the reasons I am writing of this book. And as the Bible explains, Pilate was in turmoil with his decision, and this was the beginning of the end of his reign.

Slavery and the Soul of a Nation

We live in the land of the free and the home of the brave, do we? Freedom is never free. It's so valuable. It's the only thing I can think of where the physical costs at times seems to far outweigh the moral benefit. But it's a great awakening to the conscience and convictions of who we are as a people and a nation.

The bloodshed and the untold sacrifice that has been made for our rights is staggering. Have you ever been to Arlington Cemetery? We will never understand the value of freedom until we realize what life would be like without it. From bill of rights to the emancipation proclamation, it's obvious to me that this country is the safest place for freedom on earth. But freedom from what? If just from the slave trade since the beginning of time when a people would invade another culture, the people who were defeated became the slaves of the victor. In Leviticus 18, God warns the Israelites not to partake in the immoral act of the people whose land the Israelites are going to conquer. It would be good to note that in many instances the invasion was because of a moral decline of the people and the society that was invaded. Listen to Leviticus 18:28 in the Amplified Bible, "For the land has become defiled; therefore I have brought its punishment upon it, and the land vomits out its inhabitants."

And as far as any human atrocities, color is not an issue, black on black, white on white, person to person, and self to self; the effects of slavery are the same.

We as individuals are enslaved to ourselves in that as Romans 3:10 (NKJ) says, "As it is written there are none righteous no not one." But the freedom from self, I think, is where we need to take this fight if we are going to be truly free, first as a person, then as a society, then as a nation.

If you are a slave to your past, your conscience will not allow you the freedom the future may hold for you.

As a nation, we need to consider the sacrifice of the past and the price paid for our freedom so we can move on.

The price that was paid for our freedom alone should make us seek reconciliation with one another. We in good conscience should never allow those who gave their lives for them to die in vain. Think of the civil war.

Just as a note, if you're not a Christ follower, I warn you that if you do look at Jesus, the true slave who paid the ultimate price, your convictions will be challenged and what you believe about yourself may be drastically altered.

I believe that what has happened is we are slaves to the thinking of what others believe without consulting ourselves, a form of self-induced slavery. Why we just take what others believe and adopt it as our own is to ignore the freedom that was paid for so we can know and experience that certain inalienable right that we were endowed by our Creator. It is the worst form of bondage or slavery.

Set my people free, Moses echoed God's demand for his people in the Old Testament. I believe it is his heart's cry today and will be until we learn the human race is exactly that, a race to finish well. But for who your race is run will determine the value of you reward.

Jesus, the True Slave

I guess some statements deserve explaining. In Philippians 2:7 (NKJV), the Bible describes Jesus as a bond servant, humble and completely obedient. Now almost every definition I found for bond servant finalizes with the word *slave*. So the question is, to whom is he a slave? Well, he is a bond servant/slave to us to carry the burden that life leaves us with that we cannot carry ourselves. This is the gospel. He said, "Come unto Me all you who are weary heavy laden and I will give you rest" (Mathew 11:28, KJ21). "For My yoke is easy and My burden is light" (Matthew 11:30, KJ21). That yoke is a yoke of slavery to help carry all the burdens in life we can't carry on our own. And he does that for our benefit.

Seemingly the intention of every slave owner was to have the slave take on all the things he could not do alone for his success and benefit without cost to himself. Without cost to himself! So who pays the price for this injustice? Only a willing, humble, completely obedient slave who chose his own yoke of slavery and who was willing to endure a life of rejection and cruelty being separated from his family to spend his life working for the benefit of his owners and who after going through that made this his life's purpose to forgive the persons responsible for these acts and not hold them accountable, continuing to serve until his owners are convinced his life is a sacrifice for their success with perfect submission. Unfair you say? Now no human being chooses slavery and very few forgives. So if Jesus, the true slave, can forgive us for everything we make him carry for our benefit, why are we struggling with forgiving each other for our past? Could it be that we are in bondage to ourselves? With unforgiveness, everyone has a reason to hate. Forgiveness is the only thing that sets freedom in motion. The real question is, do we love to hate more than we like to forgive? Please ask yourself that question. If the answer is yes to hate, then you are a slave owner.

You own your own sin. So why not let Jesus, the true slave, carry that burden for you? Let's take the soul of our nation out of the hands of the slave owner.

Sacrifice

Since the beginning of time, sacrifice has been the norm for a better life. We sacrifice our time, money, energy, and ourselves to experience freedom in one form or another. We work extra hours, do odd jobs, and save for that big vacation. We give up things in one area to gain in another. It just seems everything has a price.

Ever since man has decided that he could do things better his way and not depend on God's laws, the return on his sacrifice has become less.

How many people have you spoken to lately that admit life is getting harder and harder as time goes on?

As morals and ethics decline, the price of happiness goes up. To make good moral choices is getting harder. And the price for those choices are for some too costly. They won't let go of what they can't own. You can't own happiness. Happiness is a choice. So they chase the proverbial carrot for the pleasure of a false social security and make bad choices. Just recently, I was in line at a bagel shop in town, and in front of me were two women. The one woman asked if her children were going to attend CCD classes. The woman's response broke my heart. She said, "No, my children don't attend religious classes anymore. It's to conflictive. I have not been able to get her words out of my head."

As we sell our soul in the marketplace of social acceptance, our values decline; our values and integrity are challenged. The price for peace goes up, and our morals are compromised. And so we pay the price, sometimes monetarily, sometimes emotionally, sometimes mentally but always decisively.

So when does it become worth it to sacrifice for what we know is right? You can let your conscience be your guide or your convictions be your judge, but you should never get to a point where your conscience is your judge. And for some, it's too late. They confuse convenience with good judgment. But the price they pay and the costs that are acquired at the hands of poor judgment are paid out in real-time life situations. And when life becomes anything but peaceful, guilt is the product of these choices unless we choose to ignore the truth, not to take responsibility and ignore the consequences. But be sure the price for these bad choices are far greater than the cost for making the good ones.

I think it safe to say that emotional pain can far outweigh physical pain. This is what Jesus was saying when he said, "If your hand causes you to sin cut it off it is better for you to enter into life maimed rather than having two hands to go to hell into the fire that shall never be quenched" (Mark 9:43, NKJV). I think many of us might agree that it's better to lose a hand than to be tortured emotionally for all eternity or for the rest of your life for making a bad decision. He was not saying to cut off your hand. He was making a point. Who wouldn't choose making a good moral decision in lieu of paying emotionally for the rest of your life? And all of us have made decisions that were very costly. I'm sure you have made a few. The self-injury/cutting we see today has its roots in the individual unable to deal with the emotional letdown life has left them with. They understand what Jesus meant. In the scripture mentioned above, when we are emotionally bankrupt, we are willing to go through physical sacrifice. The cross is the best example of that.

Just ask someone who has a wayward child. There is nothing these parents wouldn't sacrifice to see their child be able to overcome these mistakes. The emotional pain can be overwhelming. They would do anything to take their child's place.

Love is the most powerful force in the universe; it's the power of love that moves us to sacrifice. So in this, we get a snapshot of God's love. The emotional pain of a parent for a suffering child is the only place that we can know true compassion where your will is offered as a sacrifice to the power of love. And that's God's heart for us. He was only able to relate to the human pain of sin by watching his child Jesus take our place as a man and suffer rejection and death. In this his sacrifice, his Father's heart was moved with compassion for us. The only way a righteous God could have compassion on sin was to watch his Son feel the effects of it on us through his Child. Talk about *sacrifice*.

Which one of your children do you want to see pay the full penalty for a wrong that was not their fault? Have you ever had to watch your child suffer unjustly in a divorce or some love affair or falsely accused and were made to pay a price? If you have more than one child and you were forced to choose one to suffer unjustly, which one would that be? That was the choice God was left with, knowing the full effect of the suffering sin brings to people.

We are all God's children, and his Son became a man so that justice, compassion, and mercy was presented to the judge at the time of judgment. This compassion compels him to find a reason for his Son's sacrifice, or his death would have been in vain.

God will not let that happen, and you are the answer to his fulfillment.

God is holy and must judge sin righteously. He will always accept repentance but not rejection. The price was too great. God's answer for sin is death. It's just and right; if not, then Hitler gets a free pass. So don't let his Son die in vain. Answer the Father's call. Do it today, and tomorrow will bring promise for you and your children. Or don't and someday life at times will become unbearable without much hope for tomorrow. But that decision is yours, not God's. He already did more than he had to. The soul of the nation hangs in the balance.

Chapter 4
Are You More Valuable to Yourself or Others?

I wonder how many breakthroughs in the fields of medicine, the sciences, agricultural engineering, and social development are or were lost to apathy. In *The Traveler's Gift* by Andy Andrews, there is a chapter where an angel walks the traveler through a warehouse full of unused ideas and breakthroughs that were never able to be claimed because of apathy. There were some engineering feats beyond the imagination. The untapped potential was staggering. There was the cure for cancer and untold breakthroughs in the field of the sciences. It left you to question how many of the most important breakthroughs the world has ever seen may have been left on the shelf of the past and may never be able to benefit mankind.

I have always questioned why tragedy seems to strike in the lives of the most unlikely people. Some of the most famous, gifted, and talented people in society has had the privilege to have. I think of the overdoses, suicides, accidents, and unexplained tragedies of the sixties that took the lives of some of the most amazing talent of that era. I think of Jimmy Hendrix, Janice Joplin, Jim Morrison, Ellen Naomi Cohen (better known as Mama Cass), Greg Allman, Kurt Cobain, and more recently Robin Williams, and the list continues. Now I know that a wild lifestyle can contribute to their problems in some cases but is not the underlying cause. The empty place that fame leads us to is sometimes overwhelming. Is it a combination of brilliance and talent that makes one unable to deal with the reality of life? Or is the untimely fame an emotional overdose that pushes these beautiful people to the end? I imagine that the emotional rat race that is attached to that level of social status can easily lead to the need for clinical help. To be forced to be someone your character can't keep up with can derail a lot of people and is to the human spirit a silent killer. But the way we influence others is where we gain significance and prove to ourselves that life has meaning.

The potential of the human spirit is amazing. Some of the great achievements of the last one hundred years have been by some great and some not-so-great people, meaning that their social status was not the determining factor in their successes. But their willingness to take the proverbial leap of faith or to just put one foot in front of another is what allowed providence to take over. Jeff Bezos, founder of Amazon, at thirty years old had an idea and funded the company with his own savings or Mark Zuckerberg who at nineteen founded Facebook. We will always have successors but not necessarily forerunners. Let me say that again. We will always have successors but not necessarily forerunners. And for certain individuals, the providential things in life are just under the surface of who they are. The low-hanging fruit of success seems to be readily available. And to others, it becomes a never-ending battle for truth. But why? The answer to that question is somewhere in the human spirit of all of us who share the same world we live in today.

If we were all able to live up to our full potential in life, think of where this world would be without the encumbrances, opposition, and the disappointments that life brings. But I don't care if your name is Bezos, Zuckerberg, or Gates. We all have a date with destiny. There's a time to live and a time to die. And that time between birth and death can either change the world you live in or be a never-ending search for significance.

So what makes some overachievers and others underachievers? It's my opinion that it's more motivation than qualification. Henry Ford said, "Whether you think you can or whether you think you can't you're probably right." Everyone has the unique ability to relate to life in a way that no other person can. And their true potential is unique to who they are. Whether that potential is unlocked or not depends on character, influence, and decisions and should not be left to chance, but let there be no doubt it is there in every one of us. A prime example of this is Dr. Ben Carson who grew up in poverty and became a world-renowned surgeon and Adolf Hitler who was highly educated and attended seminary. The shocking truth is, one brought life out of poverty, the other death out of privilege. From two juxtaposed lifestyles, one saved many lives, and the other took many lives. Anybody besides me puzzled? The real problem is they both believed that their purpose was for betterment of mankind. Listen to what the Bible says about what is in the heart. "The human heart is deceitful above all things and desperately wicked; who know it?" (Jeremiah 17:9, AMP). So how can we trust ourselves when we decide to take a stand on what we may believe is right? The plain truth is we can't. There is no formula to follow that will assure us that what we believe and what we stand for will promote good will and benefits those who look up to us for who we are. I think of Jim Baker, Jimmy Swaggert, Bill Clinton, and the list goes one. Any rational person who knew and believed in the purposes of these individuals knew their intentions were initially pure and good.

So what happened? Misplaced trust. Misplaced trust is the breeding ground for deception. To trust in *yourself* instead of the purpose you were called for misplaces authority and is the avenue to failure.

There is a valuable life lesson here I think we all need to learn. Legacy and influence are closely related, and how we value ourselves will be judged by the example we leave to those who follow us. Everyone is remembered for something. And some things we never forget.

The precept I like is *humility is power under control.* Humility without purpose or authority is not humility but brokenness. To be humbled, there has to be a willingness to relinquish authority or sacrifice for the benefit of others. To lose something of no value is not humility. Some good examples of humility (power under control) are Jesus, Joseph, Moses, and John the Baptist. They each knew their God-given purpose; they had a choice yet yielded their purpose for an ultimate cause.

Good leadership should be humility (power under control) under authority. The ability to relinquish that power to authority is how good leadership thrives. There is an inexhaustible source of potential that every visionary is aware of when they are able to relinquish power or control to the purpose they were called to. It's a hallmark of faith. And as every Bible believer knows, every circumstance of life can be found in that book. So here is the biblical interpretation to the above. Jesus said in John 7:18 (AMP), "He who speaks on his own accords seeks glory and honor for himself. But he who seeks the glory and the honor of the One who sent him, he is true and there is no unrighteousness or deception in him."

So if you "trust in the Lord with all thine heart and lean not unto thine own understanding in all thy ways acknowledge Him and He will direct thy paths" (Proverbs 3:5–6, KJ21), it's hard to misplace trust.

To follow or adopt a lifestyle of someone who we highly regard and respect can be detrimental to the faith we put in mankind. Let me explain. There are thousands of people who have abandoned their faith in God due to the bad choices of some prominent people of influence in their lives. There are very few people that have had an exemplary role in my life that after knowing all the good, bad, and ugly things that life has brought them through would make me want to trade places with. After finding out what it took to get them where they are today, I have to say, "I would opt for my own experience." Who would want to trade places with Jesus? Before you answer that or think you would, you should take a good look at the emotional cost beside the physical price. I believe the emotional letdown from false accusations and betrayal had just as much of an impact, if not more, than the physical pain, hence the sweating drops of blood. But the truth is, we cannot be anyone but who we are. Just let that sink in for a moment. In the Bible, King David tried on King Saul's armor before he went out to defeat Goliath. It was a terrible fit. The way our character rises to life's situations and the attitude we take toward the pros and cons of life determines whether we fail or succeed. So you really are stuck being you. The determining factor for who you are is not in the lives of other people. Now their examples may be influential, but we cannot reproduce circumstance. Circumstance is what happens in time as we move forward with our goals and values to achieve an end result. The circumstances of life cannot be changed or controlled by preplanning, doing the right things, making wise choices, or by listening to the way someone approaches life's problems. Our circumstances in life may be similar with regard to people, places, and things but never with regard to the things we can't control. We plan. We prepare. We save and then! Just fill in the blank. Anybody with me?

Anybody ever plan a wedding? There are no books or an event-planning strategy that can prepare you for the circumstances that will occur on that day. I remember my granddaughter's wedding. There were people from three states that were traveling long distance to be there, and the day before the wedding we had the biggest and only snowstorm of the year, eighteen inches plus. The wedding was beautiful, but I don't think anyone expected that set of circumstances.

I'm sure there is wisdom to be found in the life experience of others, but our lives are unique, not universal. When the time comes to reconcile your checkbook, you can't borrow from Peter to pay Paul. The name on that account is you. So the question is, can you reconcile your failures with your decisions and get a positive net result? Or do you operate in the negative?

From your fingerprints to the hairs on your head, you are one of a kind. So what have you done with who you are? I know these questions are probing, and I hope I don't lose some of you here, but you won't be left wanting. This will not be a dead end. I promise.

We all need to be acknowledged and affirmed first by others and then by ourselves. Without the acceptance of others, our lives become aimless, and we will be forced to search for a path and a purpose that reveals our identity. Lately, the question I've been asking is, are we to a point in our culture where nobody cares about life and purpose? I don't believe that to be true, and that kind of thinking will allow us to sit on the shelf and watch time go by while other people make decisions for us. This may be okay for toddlers, but before too long, they, too, want to leave their mark. However, today just ask anybody who they would like to be. And now, more than ever before, the underlying message is anybody but me. But why? Why are we in such an identity crisis? It is true that when left to ourselves, we are like pilgrims on a journey to find hope and purpose for our souls. A newborn left alone without attention will eventually die of a broken heart. The deprivation of a lonely heart will drain your energy and purpose, will leave you desperate, and like a plant without sun, it will wither and die. We all need nurturing. But in life unless you find significance and purpose in who you are and know what you are living for, it will always be harder to let go of the things that hold you back. Never knowing how to determine what avenue to take or how to choose the thing that will promote our potential has left many of us to a blind leap of faith. The Bible mentions the penalty of the lack of knowledge and vision, and it's no wonder that the world we live in has lost its way and is desperate for truth, for without truth, knowledge is folly and wisdom is foolishness where purpose is lost and life is a game.

However, we were never meant to go it alone.

Dr. Henry Cloud in his book *The Secret Things of God* cites a study done on cortisol, a stress hormone. In the study, while monitoring the cortisol level of a primate, they piped in loud music. And as you would expect, it's cortisol level was through the roof. Then they put another primate in with it.

Well, primate number one's cortisol level dropped dramatically, proving we were meant to share our burdens with each other at deep levels. We are not made to go it alone. But although we need the influence, guidance, and support of others, our circumstances draw us away from the pack, and we are left to our own devices with our convictions to make choices based on our experience or make a judgment call as to what we think is best, some easy choices and some not so easy. I remember having to make some decisions as to what treatment my wife would choose for cancer. The life-or-death choices are the ones that try our souls, and to be able to make those choices with peace of mind is hopefully where we will all be someday, left to use life's best lessons to help us make choices we can live and die with. Easier said than done you say. Well, the odds are, we will all have to make that decision if not for a loved one, for ourselves. But to look at life with the attitude that it all works out in the end, "don't worry, be happy" is a recipe for the apathetical tertiary overtaking this society. The disappointments in life are a breeding ground for hopelessness that awaits every one of us as circumstance and reality collide. Life is not easy, and what you don't know can hurt you. To be able to make good decisions in trying times depends on what we know about life and ourselves, our level of purpose, fulfillment, and our attitude. The "I don't care" way of thinking is a delusional trap that leads to despair or worse.

A guideline I use that allows me some solace is that God doesn't care what you *think* until *you know how much he cares*. Let me say that again. God doesn't care what you *think* until *you know how much he cares*. What we think very rarely is reality, especially if you are a believer in the *good news*. God does not judge us on our thoughts but on our intentions. If we were judged on our thoughts, the guilt would be unbearable, and I'm sure this has overtaken the best of us at times and has a lot to do with the hopeless state that many of us find ourselves in. But God's grace is the antidote, and his forgiveness is the remedy. So when you know how much he cares, it doesn't matter what you think simply because whatever you think, good or bad, positive or negative, it cannot change the way he loves you.

I never like to continually go back on stats that are difficult, but again while writing this chapter, there were three more suicides. A person of fifty-seven made his decision to end his life. A young teen of a radio host ended life by overdose, and more recently, a thirty-six-year-old father of two went missing and after three days was found in a lake with his ankles tied together and weighted as he walked in the thin ice. If anyone can find it within themselves to think that under the right circumstances these decisions may have been the right ones, this is why this chapter is written. We all at one time in life have hit rock bottom.

It seems that the ability to be able to sustain self-acceptance and happiness is not attained by knowledge, social status, net worth, fame, fortune, luck, good looks, or good parents but by who we are and what value we possess that will influence others because the influence we have on others is the cornerstone of a healthy personal experience. I'll bet primate number two left the cage with more self-esteem than what he came with.

To be led to believe you're useless to yourself and to others is the excuse for the apathy that has infiltrated the human spirit of many of us today. We give up and believe that we are who we are and can never change, just a nobody. But the urge to be recognized cannot be suppressed indefinitely. So we act out on whatever we feel is right without regard for anyone or anything. If you doubt that, watch the news or pick a local newspaper, if you dare. Acting out or making a statement is a cry from the depths of one's soul to be recognized and to feel like you make a difference. We all need to be noticed, and everyone needs recognition, but today because of the depravity of the human spirit (the inability to know right from wrong or admitting to it), hopelessness is on a collision course with reality.

We have become so desperate for purpose and fulfillment that we are compelled to take drastic measures under false pretenses. To say this has reached epidemic proportions, I wish, was an understatement. If you choose to deny the facts, I recommend you watch the nightly news, read the newspaper, go back and read chapter one, or like some in the NFL, just take a knee!

Lately, there has been a drastic rise in divorces in older couples. The emptiness that a life without purpose can lead to is a social disease that has been at the forefront of many of these divorces. We try to free ourselves from boundaries both good or bad only to find that we are in bondage to who we are. Acting out of a lack of significance can only lead to an unending search for fulfillment. And after a few encounters with reality without a healthy perspective can lead to depression or a fleeting desire for something new. The divorce statistics are staggering, and at the end and sometimes when it's too late, we wind up with a reality breakdown. To be unable to deal with reality has undermined the integrity of our society as a whole. I have spoken to numerous individuals who have been married one or more times and sadly are still as unstable as ever. I hope this is hitting home for some of us.

The influence we deposit in others and the freedom at which we can do it is the greatest catalyst for self-worth I know of. Ask any teacher, parent, coach, pastor, trainer, or writer. It is key to finding significance. But unfortunately, it is only experienced by few. To be able to be an agent for change when there are no options but despair or be the bearer of good news when the chances are slim has to be the number one message of eighty percent of all novels and motion pictures ever written. The narrative of good over evil is as old as man himself and is a reminder of the eternal hope residing in the heart of every human spirit. As they say, "hope springs eternal."

However, hope deferred makes the heart sick, and because of the social injustices of today, we are lead to believe that who we are and what we believe has little worth since in the end all will be lost. Well, you may think I am exaggerating, but I have noticed a trend to evil triumphing over good on many fronts. It's been a natural progression to today's thinking. And who knows what else is stolen by the false pretenses that we have allowed to influence both young and old. We will never know the influence, insight, and wisdom of those lives short-circuited by never wanting to take the next step. Just as in *The Traveler's Gift*, those breakthroughs will forever be left on the shelf of history. A legacy lost can be the tragedy found in the headlines of today.

So what is the answer? Are there guidelines that transcend circumstances? Are there proven practical principles that we can follow? A path to peace, truths that transcend time that cannot be shaken?

When God created man/woman in his image, I don't think he left much out. I am amazed at the feats of some athletes. It's almost supernatural the abilities some of them possess. And time and again, these records are broken. The definition of a miracle is an amazing accomplishment not normally achieved by natural circumstances. I think of David Tyree of the New York Giants when he caught the Super Bowl winning pass. He acknowledges a divine intervention. And isn't that what we want? To see something out of the norm. And yet we do all we can to dismiss divine intervention in the things that make us believe that we are made in God's image, unless we believe that man is god as some do. The limitation to that kind of thinking is that it always leaves an emptiness.

Let me explain. You can attribute a physical accomplishment to good health, skill, dedication, hard work, and tenacity. But these attributes are fast fleeting, hence NFL not for long. I think of Mohammad Ali, the greatest boxer of all time. In his prime, he was amazing. I recently saw a documentary of him and how the effects of Alzheimer's left him less than what any of his fans would want to see. So the human experience is limited not only by time but by chance. Hence, let us eat, drink, and be merry for tomorrow we die. And for some, maybe tomorrow can't come soon enough.

No, I think we were made with the hope of eternal security to find the one thing that will not disappoint. And those who are searching soon find out it is not of this world.

And So the Search Continues

A self-defeating mind-set that can never be satisfied, like the zombies portrayed across the media, we become the living dead.

I believe it is a taste of what Jesus meant when he was talking about hell, and I'll paraphrase, "In that place there will be weeping and gnashing of teeth."

The truth about the human spirit is we are goal oriented, driven by the ability to live up to who we want to be, a force for good. And depending on our convictions, willingness to live and die for the truth we know, we usually accomplish this by good deeds or hard work. We believe the reward will far outweigh the effort. So we are created to expect to be justified in our efforts. Most people will tell you that they are going to heaven because of what they have done. Then in the same breath, they deny there is a God or hell. The problem is you can't have it both ways. And your conscience demands an answer. So we instinctively believe in heaven and want to deny hell. It can't work that way and will lead to the struggle for the peace we all need within ourselves.

Possible but Not Reasonable

In the book *Cold Case Christianity*, J. Werner Wallace explains the conflicts and differences between possibility and rational reason. As he explains, the possibilities in a court case are endless, but the jurors are asked to find a verdict beyond reasonable doubt and not on possibilities but evidence alone. Although we as human beings are created with a hope in endless possibilities, to judge things reasonably without considering the possibilities does not come natural to us.

But beyond a reasonable doubt can be a cornerstone of justice when it comes to life or death. And so we should make it a habit to put reason ahead of doubt. It's been my experience and the experience of untold others that when God says, "Come now let us reason together," reason becomes the catalyst beyond the shadow of a doubt that will bring enough evidence to set the captive free from the lies we allow ourselves to believe. But the belief in an all-knowing, all-powerful God is a stumbling block to some and a hindrance to many of us Christians and non-Christians alike if we were honest with ourselves.

My wife had a sign on the wall in my office that read, "Coincidence is when God does a miracle and decides to remain anonymous." But when the hope we are endowed with is allowed to be overshadowed by endless possibilities, we tend to be blind to have faith in the truth. I guess that's why Lady Justice wears a blindfold. But then again, I don't think women need to see to know. No offense to you, women, it's better than having excellent eyesight as most men claim and not being able to get the picture. It's like my wife says, "It's right there," and almost without thinking, my response is, "Where?" I am learning to look before I think or speak. And so far, so good.

One of my first jobs as a young hippie was a Good Humor ice-cream man. I think the title (Good Humor man) has stuck with me. The Bible says that laughter is like a medicine. In studies the health benefits to laughter are astounding; it can actually improve your health. It draws people together in ways that bring healthy physical and emotional changes in the body. So if you're older and didn't think that was funny, think about the alternative. To look at all the evidence before making a rational decision is something we say we can't afford, especially in this fast-paced world we live in. But whatever the sacrifice, we must. The influence we will make on those who look to us as an avenue of hope is what can be a lifeline that will give a reason to turn evidence into faith.

Our value and the hope locked up in all of us can be summed up in this equation: Self-worth = who you are to God × your influence on others.

It is a valuable lesson to all of us.

But if who you are to your self does not have any value to you, then your self-worth is dependent on others unless you find out you are worth more to God than you think. He thinks so. So why not ask? His opinion can make you a world changer.

Chapter 5
Truth, Denial, and Deception

Some Thoughts on Truth

Truth can't be judged; it's too plain. The trial of Jesus before Pilate has more implications than seen at face value. Although Pilate knew Jesus was being falsely accused, Jesus was insistently truthful with him. When he asked Jesus if he was a king, Jesus agrees with him but lets him know his kingdom is not of this world, eliminating the accusations of an insurrection against the Romans which was what the Jews were accusing him of. Jesus answered, "My kingdom is not of this world. If it were, my servants would fight to prevent my arrest by the Jewish leaders. But now My kingdom is from another place" (John 18:36, NIV). "You say correctly I am a king for this I have been born and for this I have come into the world came into the world, to testify to the truth. Everyone who is of the truth hears My voice" (John 18:37, NASB), making himself the source of truth. Pilate knew the truth about the innocence of Jesus, yet he didn't know what truth was even though it was standing right in front of him. The question that every judge has to ask himself was his reply. What is truth? Pilate knew he was innocent and continued to try to convince the mob but to no avail. He was afraid of convicting an innocent man, so he washed his hands of his blood. He also knew that one cannot judge innocence. I have always wondered if Pilate will be in heaven. He treated Jesus with more respect than most people today do.

The point is, he could not judge truth because truth is innocent. Man cannot judge truth; if that were possible, truth would be relative, left to man's interpretation, making man a god unto himself. And if man would have judged God, *as in Pilate's case*, if what Jesus said about himself was not true, then the gospel would have no power over us, but you can't judge the truth. For man to judge God would be the same as a chicken asking an egg what its purpose is. However, many of us don't recognize the truth even when it is standing right in front of us, which was the case with Pilate.

Truth is present when reality and circumstance collide. When the reality and circumstances of life become overwhelming, truth is the antidote. In some cases, when the truth needs to be revealed for the greater good, it is sometimes precluded by an accusation or a doubt about the facts. But the truth reveals what the accusation conceals. I'll say that again. The truth reveals what the accusation conceals. Accusations may be based on anger, a grudge, or to cover up the truth due to guilt. That's why in our legal system we are innocent until proven guilty.

Because of our tarnished view of what truth is due to our human nature, we will most likely believe the accusation. The more we are able to relate ourselves to the accusation, the more likely we are to side with the accuser. Let me say that again. The more we are able to relate ourselves to the accusation, the more likely we are to side with the accuser. It takes one to know one. Sounds familiar, the double standard of most accusers. Jesus never held back the truth by calling these people that they were hypocrites. However, the truth is plain, and because of that, truth is an innocent judge. And only by judging based on the truth can any judge find himself innocent as to the sentence of the person found guilty. Please pray for our judges.

Truth is benign in its purpose; it has no agenda.

Truth stands like a tower over reason in the spirit of every human. It's where the conscience can judge itself and find peace. Truth is the verdict that sets us free and gives us permission to characterize our lives. It's in the truth that significance finds its reward. Truth has no agenda. It's up to us. We either accept it or reject it. If you believe that truth is relative, then this is all semantics to you, and we will cover the effects of denial in the remainder of this chapter.

It can't be denied; it's too overwhelming.

Confessing the truth has the power to end strife. It puts an end to confusion. When faced with the truth, you are compelled to conform to the truth or rebel. But it can't be denied.

Truth can't be eliminated; it's the foundation for reason.

People don't want to be bothered with things that take up time without a purpose. They want to know what your purpose is. They want to know you have a reason for doing what you do. When they find out there is some truth to what you are doing, they are compelled to search out that truth to a reasonable end.

Truth can't be dismissed or ignored. When the truth is established, a reasonable end is unavoidable. Only in truth can the blindfold of Justus be removed without prejudice.

Truth can't be ignored without consequences.

If it's true you have cancer, you had better not ignore the facts.

If you witness a crime or know of a wrongdoing and you ignore it, you may be an accomplice. And your penalty may be as severe as the person or persons committing the act. To ignore the truth has consequences, and the further away from the truth we get, the more complicated life becomes. Listen to Ecclesiastes 8:11 (AKJV), "Because sentence against an evil work is not executed speedily, therefore the heart of the sons of men is fully set in them to do evil." Please allow me to rephrase this. Because the parents have not dealt with sin quickly, the children will now pay the price. We are witnessing the truth and the consequences of that scripture as it unfolds today.

Truth is the foundation of justice.

Justice has no value without truth. The rights and wrongs of a society not based on truth is a destructive and a divisive force. The founding principles of a nation that are not founded on truth will become unstable. Today's news is a testimony of this.

Truth is what holds fact and reason together.

Facts will always search for a reason. In a court case when the facts are known, we are compelled to search for a reason. Like the shootings in Los Angeles, everyone is asking why. They are still looking for a reason as to why this man acted out in this way. When the truth is known, the search is ended. The facts and reason bring an end to the question why.

Truth always makes sense.

It always is wise to act on truth. To act on a falsehood will end up costing you emotionally, mentally, relationally, or monetarily.

Truth increases awareness.

When you are aware of the facts and you know the truth, you get a picture of where you should go next.

Truth uncovers guilt.

When the facts leave you at a place where there is no longer a reason to doubt, the implications are exposed. To deny the facts can expose an ulterior motive to overshadow the truth. The only reasons to hide from the truth is guilt, shame, or contempt.

Truth makes a way for freedom.

To admit the truth when you have done something wrong sets the prisoner free. I'm sure there are people in prison who are guilty and are not struggling with their guilt any longer because they have faced the truth. And just the same, there are people who are free who can't handle life because of their inability to admit to their wrongdoings or to find a place to forgive those wrongs done to them. You can walk through life in prison to your guilt, or you can live in a confined space with the peace that passes all understanding. Truth is the great emancipator. The peace we find within will someday far outweigh the things in life that temporarily remove us from reality. The only way to deal with a reality crisis will always be the truth.

It's a fact of life.

It's a fact of life that people who deal with truth and live their lives perusing it live a stressless life.

Some More Facts on Truth

There is no justice without it.
Because justice can only live for the truth, the truth will prevail.
The just will live by faith!
You know it when you hear it.
You don't have to see it to know it and is the hope of every visionary.
It's an absolute founded on its own merit.
It makes sense out of nonsense.
It's worth more to the innocent.
It's a revelation of hope to the offended.
It gives sight to the blind.
Truth exposes the lie.
It's rest for the soul.
It brings peace of mind.
Truth lays your doubts to rest.
Truth transforms doubt into peace.
It leads captivity captive.
Without it, facts are baseless.
Truth always points in the right direction.
It's a lighthouse to the soul.
It's the reason for liberty.
It's the song of the redeemed.
It's at the heart of a nation.
It should never be taken lightly.
It convicts the skeptic.
Truth is blind to the accuser.
We should let the truth be told.

It can't be purchased.

It's the price for freedom.

Children love to hear it.

It clears your mind.

It makes life worth living.

It can be a cure for disease.

It always helps to know it.

Truth promotes decision.

It eliminates trivia.

It's peace of mind to a judge.

It pays to tell the truth.

Truth stands alone in its purpose.

It promotes freedom of expression.

It's the search of the pilgrim.

It can't be reversed.

Truth is the reason for an acquittal.

You can count on it.

It's the compass for a journey.

It doesn't have an end but is an end in itself.

It's eternal.

It's really all that matters.

It transcends time.

Truth is solitary in itself but inclusive to all.

You can know the truth.

When you know it, it will set you free.

Truth reveals reality.

It silences the accuser.

Without it, reality becomes relative.

It's sometime hard to face, but it's found in the face of God.

Truth influences all aspects of life. There is no set of circumstances that the truth can't aid. I am intrigued by the weight we put on truth. Yet it is becoming one of the rarest commodities of modern-day society. Because of the lack of truth, it is becoming harder to trust even in the closest relationships.

The level of mistrust in marriage today is at epidemic proportions. Many women say they only have limited trust in their spouse. Men can't communicate with their wives due to a fear of having to give up something. Or they chose not to because of some hidden agenda. The lack of communication is directly proportional to the absence of truth we allow.

We fear we will be taken advantage of if we are truthful. Now I'm not abdicating throwing your pearls before swine. But in a covenant relationship where love means sacrifice, truth is needed to grow trust. However, our social state has undermined truth and sacrifice. We now offer time instead of sacrifice. An offering is temporary and asks for a return. But sacrifice is the means by which a relationship will grow. The truth of the matter is without someone dying to self or sacrificing something of value, the relationship will stop growing. To give without measure is what sacrifice is all about.

Anything else is just an offering. The best illustration of sacrifice I've heard is what happens when a farmer walks into the barnyard and announces bacon and eggs for breakfast. The chicken says, "Sounds great."

The pig says, "Easy for you to say."

If our social status becomes the foundation of our relationships, we are on shaky ground. When we base our commitment on social norm, betrayal is not far behind simply because when we have our own agenda, we will look to someone or something that will justify our behavior.

Without truth, doubts and questions can lead to mistrust, and the search for answers in the wrong places can lead to unfaithfulness. I have spoken to women who were sure their spouse have betrayed them. Why? Because without truth, we can't trust. And our marriages become an institution instead of a covenant. If you have to be interrogated in order for your spouse to find out what really happened in any given circumstance, it's a sign that there is a lack of truth in your relationship. And all the women said amen. The more truth, the more trust; the less truth, the less trust. Now I know that men and women have a communication failure generally speaking, but transparent truth will build trust, unless of course we have something to hide or an agenda we feel takes precedence.

If or when you were ever married, you took your wedding vows. The odds are against you ever being able to fulfill them in our current social setting. And they become insurmountable with the absence of truth. There are just too many variables. In reality, we promised things we can't make good on. Who can know what we will be like tomorrow? And we make a promise that we are unable to keep or be truthful to.

In a Christian setting, it is my opinion the wedding vows really portray God's promise to us personally. He promises to be with us for better or worse, for richer or poorer, in sickness and in health, and even till death. If we take his promise as personal and act out on them, we will be the example to our wives of what it's like to be around him.

That's what women are really looking for anyway. To live out that promise and make it a lifestyle becomes irresistible to those we are in relationship with.

Truth is transcendent. It existed before reason, or there would be nothing for reason to search for. To deny the truth is the end of logic. To ignore the truth promotes ignorance.

Love, forgiveness, and truth are the most powerful forces in the universe. But truth is independent in itself. Love is sacrificial and takes action on our part, and so is forgiveness, but truth stands alone and is the pathway to freedom from bondage. It's the gatekeeper of life.

Liberty without truth is slavery in a sense. The liberty to be free to follow in the pursuit of happiness without truth will become endless and offers no fulfillment. To know what you believe is true should be important and should be a catalyst for your purpose in life. If not, you're in for a disappointment. And I think that the disappointments in life is what leads to the desperation of what is being played out in our society today. This should shake every parent to their core. Our children are desperate to know the truth.

Children love the truth. They are fulfilled by knowing that when they act on truth, it will always have a positive effect. If you are always truthful with a child, they will learn that they can depend on you to react to the truth in ways that will transform. To instill truth in a child at a young age will be a pathway to maturity. A healthy respect for the truth will build character, lead to integrity, and will allow them to live life to its full potential.

Once you know the truth, your response will judge your character, and your conscience or your human spirit, *the way we determine things to be right or wrong,* will determine your fate in the matter. The human spirit is what Jesus meant when he said you must be born again of the spirit. But we are always free to choose what direction we will take when we are faced with the truth. So in that respect, God will always allow us to choose what path we will take, allowing us the freedom of choice but only in the light of the truth. If you think that the truth is there to rob you of fulfilling your desires, then there is a conflict between your thoughts and your conscience. And there is no freedom in that choice. Freedom is when the will is surrendered, the mind is satisfied, and your emotions are at rest. The decisions we make out of our convictions should eliminate any questions we may have and bear witness to the truth we find within ourselves, and that is the honest truth, but the choice is ours.

But the thing I love the most about the truth and getting to know God through the gospel is that he never gives up on us. Knowing our limitations and considering our circumstances, he sends the spirit of truth, the Counselor, to convince us of our shortcomings and will never leave you in doubt until you are convinced of his goodness then takes credit for our shortcomings, something only he can do. In that, he shows us the reason we were put into that set of circumstances that caused us to go astray. It has become his purpose. That purpose is to take who he made us to be, to face the circumstances that life brings and through grace allow us to walk through them again following truth without shame or blame, facing the truth and finding freedom, exposing our nature without tarnishing the image of him we were created in till we are convinced that he and he alone deserves all of our honor and praise. I have noticed that God really only moves for two reasons—to change people and to give glory to himself. That's redemption. Hope you all got that. God is always willing to deal with our doubts and shortcomings but not with unwillingness. And that's the truth. Open the floodgates of your soul and allow the truth to set you free. Your children and all those you are in relationship with will be glad you did. Or deny it and excuse yourself from the reality of life.

Denial

Denial at its root undermines our integrity. It may be caused by guilt or the fear of paying the consequences for a wrong done to us or by us.

It is a charade played out in our psyche to avoid the penalty of a wrong done or to shift the blame, to avoid at any cost the tearing down of our humanity, so we deny the judgment of our actions by self-justification. We become a law unto ourselves. And just as in the book of Judges, everyone did what was right in their own eyes.

We rationalize our actions either by believing that what was done to those we trespass against was for their own good or somehow they deserved what was done and is a product of their behavior. When we do this, we are lying to ourselves, overshadowing the truth with a lie and damaging our character and integrity. And the end result is the death of the conscience. What this book is about is the redemption of the human spirit, getting back to the truth lost within us. Living in the shadow of a lie, *denial* will captivate the soul into false justification, making us a god unto ourselves. At which point, the rights and wrongs of life are left to the wayward thinker in order to justify whatever life brings. The purpose of life becomes empty as there is no reward for right or wrong, and feelings become more important than the truth because within this lie, truth does not exist. If it feels good, do it. It's the slippery slope that leads to hopelessness. The lie that life is not worth living is the underlying message, and reconciliation becomes foolish. Because with denial truth can't exist, the conscience is seared, leaving them incapable of ethical functioning. In 1 Timothy 4:2 (AMP), it says, "But the Holy Spirit explicitly and unmistakably declares, that in latter times some will turn away from the faith paying attention instead to deceitful, and seductive spirits, and doctrines of demons, misled by the hypocrisy, of liars whose consciences are seared with a branding iron leaving them incapable of ethical functioning."

To deny the truth imprisons the human spirit to live out a sentence of an aimless life forced to move through life as best as one can, coping with life as best as one can by any means necessary to ease the pain. The emotional pain of life far outweighs the physical. The emotional pain is permanent; the physical is temporary.

But with enough physical pain, the emotional pain can be replaced, even if only for a while. This destructive lifestyle is at the root of the cutting or worst played out in the everyday life of young people today. And denial is at its root. It's one thing to ignore the truth, but to know the truth and deny it will erode the emotional well-being of anyone held in its grip. The justification for our reasoning away from the truth will end in a breakdown of our well-being, lifestyle, relationships, and emotional stability.

Deception

Deception is the act of hiding the truth in order to gain an advantage.

The failure to admit to one's self that something is true is the by-product of deception. When someone can no longer admit to themselves that something is true, they can be controlled by any whim of doctrine society has to offer or worse. I think of Charles Manson and the Sharon Tate murders or of Jim Jones or David Koresh and the Waco Texas compound. Yet in small ways, we all fall to the deception of truthless facts being fed to us on a daily basis. Deception is at its worst when the individual is no longer dealing with reality.

When the person or movement *because of their commitment or level of involvement* has reached a place of no turning back, it is when the stakes are the highest.

At this point, whether or not there is validity in what they are doing has nothing to do with the ultimate goal. I would hate to admit that deception in big and small ways has taken more lives and is still wreaking havoc in the youth of today, but the facts stand alone. From the addict who can't cope with life to the scorn of a politician, the deception that led us to lie to ourselves is the root of the problem. On a small scale, deception can create a multitude of disorders. But in high-profile cases, the devastation affects multitudes of followers who put their trust in the deceiver. And in many cases, lives hang in the balance. Look at the stats in chapter one on suicide. Just recently in the news, there was a politician who left a suicide note and carried it out because of sexual-misconduct accusations that were debunked years ago that have surfaced again. This man was a preacher.

When public opinion outweighs the truth, deception and *believing a lie* can undermine the character of an individual. Leaving them on trial with themselves and self-condemnation is usually the verdict. The questions "Why me?" or "I hate my life" is the overall consciences of our youth. Why? Because they can't know the truth. They have been deceived.

Chapter 6
Decision, the Island We All Need to Visit

"No man is an island," a quote from a seventeenth-century author and preacher John Donne, is true. We are made to be in fellowship with one another. However, we alone are responsible for what we allow to determine our path in life. In the last chapter, we talked about truth, denial, and deception. To think that without believing in the absolutes that truth holds that denial or deception do not exist is a dangerous false premise plaguing the human spirit. Again in the context of this book, the human spirit is our conscience, *the part of us that determines what we deem to be right or wrong,* and it is that spirit that Jesus meant when he said, "You must be born again of the spirit."

The denial of the truth is the opiate of the masses that follows a self-centered humanistic approach to life. This has led to the emptiness and the depravity of the lives of many we see played out in society today. But ultimately, the fact is, the choice is ours. We are free to allow what we decide to be our judge and let our conscience be our guide. But if we never allow ourselves to question our motivation, we fall prey to our own devices and motives, creating a dangerous vacuum of self-motivated and self-proclaimed prophecy that can drive us and others in the wrong direction. No man is an island for sure. However, even though our convictions are formed by the influence and interaction with others, there is no significance in following the opinion of others without having a healthy self-evaluation. Without it, we are just pawns or puppets driven by a slave mentality or worse.

There are a lot of people today who are addicted to following the crowd. There is an unending flow of new experiences available to both the young and old. And it is easy to throw caution to the wind when we are faced with these *spur-of-the-moment* decisions that we are forced into making. Depending on how much value you place on yourself is what will allow you the freedom to make good choices at any given time. But for the most part, it's how we are viewed by others that drive these on-the-spot demands that we allow to do the bidding for our identity. Just recently there is a social-media challenge called the Tide-pod challenge where you are challenged to ingest a soap pod. This has caused sickness and death. Yet the cry to be noticed by your peers and make a statement is an identity crisis killing both young and old in massive numbers. The most recent tragedy in Florida where a nineteen-year-old killed seventeen people has shaken us to the core. And we ask why. Deep inside, this young man was a cry to be noticed, to make his mark on society, and to show everyone that he was true to himself and in what he believed, and by acting out, he was making his statement count, "Do you believe me now?" Being true to your beliefs is what fuels self-significance, and without consideration to good or evil, the effects are devastating.

Curiosity along with a longing to be accepted gives way to making wrong choices. For instance, "Hey, have you ever been to x place? Hey, try this. It's cool. I did that before. You got to try this one time. You can't pass this deal up. Don't say no. Don't be such a party pooper. What will everyone think? What will they say? It's okay. No one will know. I won't tell anybody."

Whether it's making an illegal turn, a visit to a bar, a decision on promiscuity, or simply buying a car, the view of others has played the piper, has led even the most gifted and talented of us astray, and has led to harm and even death.

But it's the lie that "no one will know" or the "I won't tell anybody" is an assault on our character. Don't believe it. It's identity theft 101. It's as if your actions won't have consequences; beware, or your ally will soon hold the keys to the freedom you gave away.

The consequence here is you are led to believe you are compromised. You didn't know what you were doing. You can't trust yourself or that this choice to act was involuntary in nature and has rendered you useless. You as an individual were devalued. Your freedom of choice was violated, and your right as an individual was usurped.

The problem is, everyone will know, but everyone will easily forget except you. And now you are left with the wages of a decision that was made for you. Your authority was usurped, and your identity was stolen. Then there are those who do remember who hold us hostage and pervert the truth.

And because it was all about you, you can be sure you will be constantly reminded and in some cases will never forget. When the smoke clears, it will be you alone that is left to pick up the pieces. And these pieces never really fit together the same as before. The *piece* that was stolen is now in the hands of the usurper, and life becomes a puzzle. Because you believe you had no say in your own decision, you are unable to get it back. The cost to redeem yourself stands in judgment of those who you allow to control you. Because you can't reconcile with yourself, you seek acceptance and forgiveness from others and in some cases will go to extremes to gain acceptance and forgiveness from someone who is unable to give you what you need, but they will accept you and expect you to come to them for what you need the most—love, acceptance, and forgiveness at any cost, and some of us pay dearly.

The problem is that they can never give you back to yourself and will remind you that it was your fault in the first place. The blame falls on you, and the battle to regain your significance is fought in every decision. Your self-trust is eroded, and making decisions becomes difficult.

We all have been forced into making decisions in life, some good, some not so good, and some that have altered our lives and those around us forever. The decisions we make are the future we walk into. They set the course of where we go from here. And the island of decision, the place we all need to visit, is just as important today as when we were last at life's crossroads. It's the only place in life where you get to choose your destiny. But we need to go there alone.

Today, before a person reaches the age of accountability, the damage done by forcing questions of morality prematurely has circumvented some valuable steps to maturity and has subverted the youth process. Without the skill needed to make clear choices, based on experience, your ability to make calculated decisions is retarded. This subversion is responsible for the many personality disorders that we deal with in society today, all contributing to the depravity of the human spirit.

Forced to make irrational decisions based on a feeling of acceptance instead of facts and truth, it will lead to a history of emotional breakdowns, dangerous territory for anyone young or old steeped in indecision, and can lead to a slave mentality.

Disappointment, if not dealt with at this level, is tolerated or accepted and leads to emptiness. To believe that life is a futile attempt to gain trust in one's self or others becomes a false narrative we follow. Yet because we are born with an innate belief that somehow, somewhere, someday things will all work out, we are destined to continue on our search for hope and significance. When we consider ourselves useless, unless we are of some use to others, we will get used. Let me say that again. When we consider ourselves useless, unless we are of some use to others, we will get used. It's the human condition. People who need people are the luckiest people in the world. Or are they? Then when the chips fall or the relationship is over, we wonder why we are to blame. Why? Because mistrust has consequences. Disappointment and rejection soon follow but not without some internal damage.

When we fail to get noticed, things get worse. Gang membership is on the rise. Isis is recruiting young people, and our youth are acting out in violent and evil ways. Why? Because the things that mattered the most were taken. They need to be noticed and to know that they matter. If that basic need is not fulfilled, it leaves our young people easy prey to those who know the value of acceptance and purpose in people. Unfulfilled, this becomes a death wish, the eroding of the conscience that holds the human spirit, *our God conscientiousness* in contempt. Instead of dying of loneliness, they are compelled to find the truth about who they are or in some cases under the judgment of their peers; end it all.

The most recent school shooting tragedy in Florida has broken the trust in our society and the hope for America. Every parent is now faced with this looming threat of this happening in their school system. But the fact is, this can happen anywhere at any time. And in the time it took for me to finish this book, it has happened again.

The youth of today and society in general have been hijacked and led into a false meaning of what life is supposed to be. And they will go to any extent to live in the alternate universe of false peace, buying happiness through acceptance at any cost.

The drug companies have never sold so many antidepressants in the history of the world. And the people dependent on this false feeling of euphoria oftentimes become addicted to any number of drugs, legal or illegal. The legalization of marijuana for recreational use is the next step to the falsification of the happy life.

Life will never be happy without self-acceptance and significance, *to be an individual with value independent of outside influence*. And to achieve that, you need to accept yourself with all the brokenness, all the shortcomings, all the flaws, all the dark places, and all the disappointments and find real acceptance in the presence of God and yourself.

If you're not a believer in God, then I have to caution you that without God, self-acceptance that is gained by judging yourself will lead to shortened relationships, disappointment, and isolation, a dangerous place to be. We will cover this in a latter chapter. Only in his unconditional love and acceptance can you find what you need to be and who you need to be to yourself.

In his book *Fathered by God,* John Eldridge explains as a rule that men walk through life with a big question mark on their chest, and their children are well aware of it. Until they ask God what he thinks of them, that question remains. And until then, their fathering is superficial.

This island of decision, as secluded as it may sound, is a place of solitude and resolution, a place where you and you alone can change the world and that of those around us.

Decisions made in haste and not from our core convictions seem trivial at face value, but once they are played out in real life, their consequences can be world changing. From buying this land for trinkets, from the natives living in America at the time to Esau losing his birthright, the trend seems to be from the seemingly insignificant things in life to what amounts to world-changing events. When decisions are made in haste, there will always be winners and losers.

With every wrong decision we make or the ones made for us, we lose self-worth. If we have no value in ourselves, we cannot allow what we have to be evaluated by others. That's slavery. Please let that sink in. And like every slave owner knows, you are there to carry out their will. The sale of your will for their opinion of you is what was forfeited. Your decision will be subject to their opinion. Because you count yourself less, you have forfeited the right to choose or make your own decision, especially if this is a lover or an iconic figure in your life. What you think will not count. Your happiness and how the world turns is subject to their opinion and acceptance of you. There are countless songs written about being a slave to love, but love has nothing to do with becoming a slave.

Real love is about sacrifice, dignity, respect, and commitment. Ask anyone married for more than forty years. Now I am in no way suggesting that just by making your own decisions that good counseling is to be avoided. But even with that, the decision is yours.

If we do not allow ourselves the time and space it takes to make good decisions, life becomes a slippery slope or a game of chance. Depending on someone or something for our physical and emotional well-being will lead to what seems like betrayal or some other form of disappointment because they are not capable of giving you what you need. When we hope against all odds, that fate will play out in our favor through our popularity with others. Let me say that especially in the *age of information* we live in, this is wishful thinking. The heart and souls of many have fallen prey to social media. Cyberbullying has cost the lives of untold thousands of people and is a social disease we have not been able to control.

Our decisions count not only for us but for all those we are in relationship with. So the older we get, the more responsibility we assume just by being in a relationship of any kind, unless of course we live on a secluded island.

The good news is it's never too late to charter a trip to the island of decision. In the Bible, God would meet special people in secluded places. But when he had to give a special revelation to the Apostle John, he was exiled to an island with no one else but God to communicate with.

We all could use a self-revealing experience to let our hair down and find acceptance in the light of our shortcomings. However, acceptance and unconditional love are not available in comparison to another's experience.

You cannot be compared to another person because their experience can never give you what you need to be true to yourself. For you to gain significance without comparison as an individual can never be found in another human being. And significance is just that, finding truth within yourself.

And to do that, you need a revelation. A revelation is something shown firsthand for the first time and is not available from anyone else.

Facts Tailored to an Experience

For some of us, we are lucky enough to get some facts tailored to our experience from our fathers or our mothers. But to be independent has a lot to do with being mature. Firsthand facts tailored to our experience help us in moments without external input, but by what some call instinct, we have revealed to us what the right choice is in a particular situation. But these experiences need not be limited to time or fate. The Bible says we have not because we asked not. And the Bible makes it obvious who we are to be asking.

Matters of the Heart

In matters of the heart, however, we need a revelation, revealing the truth and canceling out false beliefs. And when we act on what was revealed, the newness of that truth can change lives.

Finding Peace and Purpose

The fact of the matter is that the piece that was stolen by the disappointments in life that left us puzzled was originally set in place without our knowing why it was there in the first place. However, knowing what its purpose is brings peace and restores hope.

We can't know why we do what we do without a revelation. So if you don't know why that missing piece was there in the first place, it only makes sense to find someone who does. When we were made, we were born in peace.

Everyone has been captivated even if for a split second at the innocence of a newborn. And deep within, we all long to be there again. We all ooh and aww over the innocence of the moment and try to fulfill their every need. So how can that innocence be restored? When your watch doesn't tell time correctly or your car is acting up, you don't go to a the home depot. No, you go to a watchmaker or a car mechanic. So when you're broken, who do you go to? In times when we are most vulnerable, God still sees us as that newborn, and we have his full attention.

The truth is, God has an inexhaustible amount of firsthand facts. We just never ask. That's why God can always deal with human failure, but he is unable to deal with complacency.

The truth of the matter is a matter of truth.

To be honest with ourselves without outside influence can take courage and integrity. We may tend to ignore, deny, or excuse the negative and highlight the positive.

But the truth of the matter is a matter of truth. And the truth may be until we find an arbitrary lover. Our trust will not be at one hundred percent.

The more truth we allow, the more self-respect we gain. Generally speaking, when dealing with people, they are there for a certain amount of self-gratitude. Their reason may be that they are there to help you. And there is great sense of accomplishment in helping others.

But if you won't take their advice or fail to follow what they expect you should do, before too long they will tell you that you are on your own if you continue making bad choices because only you can choose. And before too long, there is no sense to continue counseling. It becomes a dead end. The love we experience from humans when you think about it is really based on terms and conditions.

But an arbitrary lover has nothing negative or positive to say. The Bible says that love endures with patience and serenity. Love is kind and thoughtful and is not jealous or envious; love does not brag and is not proud or arrogant. It is not rude; it is not self-seeking. It is not provoked [nor overly sensitive and easily angered]. It does not take into account a wrong endured. It does not rejoice in injustice but rejoices with the truth [when right and truth prevail] (1 Corinthians 13:4–5, AMP).

The word *arbitrary* means *subject to an individual's will or judgment without restriction, contingent solely on one's discretion* and is derived from a

Latin word *arbiter* that translates *judge*. In human terms, it is almost impossible to find a judge who loves you and will tolerate you with your faults. It's hard to fit in the same context. To judge someone is to point out their faults and then give your judgment. Now you may do this in a loving way, but if they don't change, there is nothing left but to hope and pray they change. Or in a case of offense, let them know what they need to do for restitution or just cast judgment and leave them to their own devices. But God, unlike humans, is just that, an *arbitrary lover. We are subject to his individual will and judgment without restriction, contingent solely on his discretion.* However, he can judge your faults and leave you out of it because he loves you and not your faults. He is the only one capable of truly separating the two.

I guess if you had to be exiled to an island, you wouldn't want any other lover to be there with you. It really has a romantic ring to it. Every human being on earth is searching for just that kind of love. However, because of the demands put on life, most honeymoons are short-lived.

God's love is not a tolerating love. It's a love that separates you from your actions. If I were to put it in human terms, it would be an involuntary excuse based on truth and not mainly on preference, appearance, or feelings. The basis for most love relationships today is a choice to tolerate someone with all their shortcomings because of status, attraction, or a feeling, and in some cases compassion. Anything else is infatuation. Because of this and the feelings we have for someone, we tend to excuse their shortcomings so as not to offend them. Human beings need a reason to love and to excuse others for their shortcomings. *God does not.* We as humans love good looks, nice gestures, kindness, commitment, fame, fortune, dedication, attention, consideration, to be noticed, preferred, acknowledged, pampered, loved, forgiven, and chosen. But God does not care about what you want until you know how much he cares. His cares and your wants are mutual in the light of the truth of who he is, but the context may be different.

God's love is powerful and is expressed in his Word. The Bible says that God can divide your soul—*your mind, will, and emotions*—from your spirit, *your conscience.* So he is able to separate *what you do* from *why you do it.* And he can discern the thoughts and intents of the heart. He knows *why you think what you think.* I hope you can follow this. Please read this again if you need to.

Listen to Hebrews 4:12 (KJ21), "For the word of God is living and powerful and sharper than any two edged sword, piercing even to the dividing of the soul and the spirit, and the joints and the marrow, and is a discerner of the thoughts and the intents of the heart." In order for someone to express love on such a level is why God needs to be an arbitrary lover.

If you could know why people *thought what they thought*, it would be impossible for you to separate *what they did from why they did it* because the thoughts and intents of the heart are usually made out of self-perseveration; you would condemn them on their thoughts alone. Isn't that how we judge ourselves? Only God can separate our thoughts from our intents. And only he knows why we do what we do.

The island of decision is freedom's safest place and is where God waits for every soul who is lost at sea. For those whose shipwrecked lives land on the island of decision, know that God is waiting there for you. And the truth is, it's never too late.

As you can see, decision should be a place for individual's isolated thought when it pertains to being true to yourself and matters of the heart. Maturity and self-respect are valuable to us as individuals and add to our value as we find our way through life. Individualism coupled with maturity are vital for healthy relationships. Without it, we are dependent on others for our significance. To depend on someone other than yourself for your emotional security is a product of indecision. The uncertainty of indecision can lead to seclusion, isolation, and apathy. But before that happens, charter a trip with the lover of your soul. The good news is that it's free, and it is freedom's safest place.

Chapter 7
Why God? Perception, Indecision, Seclusion

Perception

The way things seem to be is never the way they really are. If I ended this section with that comment, I probably would have given you enough information for you to write your own chapter on the way life really is, especially if you're married because marriage is just what it says it is, two people living in relationship to one another. The way we perceive things to be has a lot to do with our past and how we view life. A good perception of life as a whole will make the decisions we all face less burdensome. The overall view we take on life has a lot to do with how we perceive life's challenges. For example, is the cup half full or half empty? And the way we view life has everything to do with how we process the everyday trials life brings. It's the difference between being a victim of a life out of our control or being able to overcome the negative, embrace it, face reality, and make decisions that will bring about positive change.

Because as research has shown, seventy percent of all of our thoughts are negative, we tend to form a negative end result. But to use some common sense, to know these results knowing that we are seventy percent negative in our thinking makes us seventy percent wrong about how we think about ourselves. I hope I am not speaking to someone with a gambling addiction. This negative mentality is an innate trait of every human being because of what we call the evils of life.

No one will argue that life is not fair. Why is there suffering and death in this world, and why would a *good* God allow evil, suffering, and death to come into the world? Why do babies get cancer and die? Why does a mom with four healthy children die suddenly, leaving a husband and children to figure out why? Why is there human trafficking, rape, and mercy killings, murders, school shootings, and suicides in mass numbers? Explain to me why a man would kidnap a four-year-old girl and sodomize and rape her for four days and then kill her and hide the body. It's no wonder that we are seventy percent negative in our thinking. Honestly, I guess in this world we don't know what to expect. Although we may not know what to think, we can know how to think about the evils of life. I am sure there isn't anyone who is reading this book who is not familiar with the evils of life. But how we process evil in the context of our lives is what forms our approach to life. We can approach life as the luck of the draw, just a chance at a good life without any rhyme or reason, nothing to be concerned about. Things will all work out the way they are supposed to. Then the unthinkable happens.

Worldviews: How We Perceive Life

The *atheistic worldview.* Let's say for instance that you do not believe in a god or a creation concept but you do believe that life is an evolutionary process and that life and death are a part of that process. This view is held by many intelligent and respectable people. The long-held view that we evolved though the evolutionary process over millions of years has been in many circles accepted as fact but has as of late been put on hold as being factual.

Due to intelligent-design research and the new breakthroughs in DNA, the atheistic evolutionists have had to revisit some foundational core beliefs on the origin of life.

More recently, a group of worldwide prominent atheists, because of the intelligent design found in our DNA, have entertained an alien seed-pod theory.

At face value, the theory of evolution seems logical, but due to the fact that nothing they believe can be observed over time (no one was here millions of years ago), there is a disconnect to make the observations needed to call it real science. Science, as defined, is *the observation of change over time.* So the belief that humans evolved from one prehistoric life-form is just that, prehistory. You can't know scientifically or claim factual evidence that this *theory* can be proven. You wouldn't know that by the way it is taught as fact in our schools and universities. The theories of microevolution and macroevolution is the central debate of these different views. But nevertheless, it is a valid worldview. This is covered in chapter one.

So what we decide is a more fulfilling way to approach life *or what you believe* (since any view, theistic or atheistic, is just that, a belief system) is the question. But how you believe life to be will affect every decision you make when it comes to the things that count in life.

What we think about life will change with time, but how we believe life is to be takes conviction and is a matter of personal decision. You can look at life and make good observations that may warrant change. Or you can go with the flow and allow fate to determine your destiny.

I think of John Lennon's song "Imagine." In the song, we are asked to imagine a world without a heaven or hell, no countries, no possessions, no killing, nothing to live or die for, no religion. As enticing and alluring as this may sound, it is a dream and can never be a reality in this life because it's true what the Bible says that the human heart is desperately wicked. Who can know it? Now I'm sure John Lennon would say that the atrocities of life are unfair and evil at times. But as long as there are humans, there will be what most would call evil.

But would it surprise you if I told you that most prominent atheists would say that if you happen to get cancer or you have been raped or you are suicidal, it's your tough luck. That's fine, but this doesn't answer the question of where does evil come from and why is there evil and suffering in the world, questions that haunts the soul of every human being with a conscience. And that means all of us. As I mentioned before, a study done on brain neurons shows we humans differ from animals in that we have another layer of neurons that cause us to ask questions. Animals do not ask questions. So when asked a question, according to how much truth is contained in our answer will determine whether our conscience, *the gatekeeper of the soul,* will be satisfied.

Richard Dawkins, a prominent outspoken atheist, in his book *The God Delusion* is quoted as saying, "In a universe of electrons and selfish genes, blind physical forces, and genetic replications, some people are going to get hurt, others are going to get lucky, and you won't find any rhyme or reason in it, nor any justice. The universe we observe has precisely the properties we should expect, if there is at the bottom, no design, no purpose, no evil, no good, nothing but a pitiless indifference." On abortion, he stated, "With respect to those meanings of human, that are relevant to the mortality of abortion, any fetus is less human than an adult pig," leaving life to chance. He was once quoted as saying, "In effect looking at life as blind forces, and genetic replications, we really can't blame Hitler for his actions."

After a debate at a college campus, there was a question-and-answer period. A young man was asking from an atheistic point of view, "What would you say to a person who is suicidal." And their answer was, "It's just tough, you need to face the universe the way it is, and accept it with all its ups and downs. Death is just what happens in the evolutionary process."

Because without death and the survival of the fittest, as atheists will admit, evolution stops. It's what is needed for evolution to advance, and since there is no good, no evil, no justice, and no reason, we should not complain when we are the victims of these evils. So when a life is shortened for being unable to deal with these evils, they boast of their view as fact. This is why some people call this view a culture of death. In their view, if there is a god, he is a hideous being who allows these atrocities in the world he created. And if he was a loving father, who needs that type of parenting?

Listen to Richard Dawkins as he describes the God of the Old Testament, a madman in the sky just waiting for someone to trespass one of his moral laws so he can sentence them to a life of suffering and loss and eventually death.

But if asked if these evils of life are wrong, they will say, "Yes, these acts are wrong and sometimes evil." So we are asked to just dismiss any of these evil atrocities to our genetic makeup. But if you acknowledge something as being wrong, you need a standard to base right and wrong by. So is it by a human standard? And if human beings are basically good, why haven't we found the remedy or an answer for the evils of life? Why is the suicide rate growing among teens and young adults at an alarming rate? Surely, with the advances in science and human behavior, we would have by now come up with a miracle drug that would be able to wipe out the depression and hopelessness that drives people to commit the atrocities played out on a daily basis today.

Being a patient in a mental hospital in my late teens, early twenties due to drug abuse, I know firsthand the effects of antidepressants and stimulants on the mental and emotional state of an individual. I remember battling with questions like, "Why was I in a world where it seems that nothing I do is able to eliminate the questions I had about myself? Why was I unable to find anything about myself that I could call significant? Why did everything I did fall apart? Why couldn't I point to one thing that I would call good that I was able to use as a compass to follow for direction?" And the more I searched, the deeper the disappointment. I am a realist and have always been brutally honest with myself. And after being treated with Thorizine and Stelazine, two antidepressants, I came to the conclusion that these drugs were not able to erase the questions I had about my significance. And the battle rages on.

I remember the exact moment that I determined that I could find no hope in myself, in the world I lived in, and in any hope that my condition could be treated.

It was at a time when I was being treated as an outpatient, and I was admitted overnight that, if I recall, wound up being a two- or three-day stay. After your morning medications, you were not allowed in your room but encouraged to socialize with the other people on the floor. After a bad experience with a person on the floor, I opted to be a loner.

The medication was so strong that at times I was not able to function physically. So I would lie on the floor in the hallway outside my room. Out of boredom, I would attempt to count the dots in the floor tile but was never able to get past seven or eight. My attention span was blocked, and my thought process was hindered by these drugs, doing nothing for the questions I so desperately needed answers to, adding to the hopelessness of my situation. I determined there was no help for my condition. And I continued on the road to destruction. So let me say firsthand that we cannot medicate the dark side of the soul. And if these are bad genes, I'm not the only one.

I think the word *perception* and *faith* are similar in that we can look at something through two sets of lenses and formulate a conclusion on how we view the information. How we view information is filtered through preset values that may or may not be true (perception). And in these nontangible ways, faith, *a belief in something*, is how we build a presupposed outcome. That's why it's important to base our conclusions not on *what we think about life* but on *how we think life is to be*. What we think about life is based on the information we have and can change with time and circumstance.

But *how we think life is to be* is a matter of the convictions of the heart that is alive with the possibilities of life versus *what we think about life,* a preconceived notion that life is a set of circumstances that cannot change.

The atheistic worldview is based on *what* we think about life and not *how* we believe life is to be. Because with an atheistic worldview, if how we believe life is to be was able to change the outcome of life's circumstances, it would be like cheating fate. In their view, you cannot alter your destiny. What you do has nothing to do with what will happen to you in life.

No matter what behavior pattern you choose, these two words are important. So just as what you think about life leaves you without any options, *how* you believe life should be leaves you open to endless possibilities and potential for change. It's really what faith is about and is the natural progression for human thought, or we would still be stuck in the dark ages not by asking *why not* but *why*. Who in their right mind would not choose possibility and potential over the unknown? Hope you can grasp this concept. Hope I haven't lost you in this, but in my opinion, this devalues our significance as human beings. Henry Ford said, "Whether you think you can or whether you think you can't, you are probably right." The possibilities of life that change by a behavior modification are endless. But you first have to believe it's possible.

Although the atheistic worldview has no answer for why there is evil in the world, nevertheless, the human spirit in all of us compels us to take a stand. But more importantly, if the atheists are to say that the evils we see in the world are wrong, they need a standard by which something is measured or a standard of what they can call good. Because if there is no good, there can be nothing bad. You just can't have one without the other. If there is a force for good, you need something to compare it to. So by what or whose standard do we deem something good? Is man's goodness the standard, or is there a universal law in authority?

If there is a law, there has to be a lawgiver. Humans are not capable of making their own laws governing a standard of life to be lived by, just read your history books.

So man is not a good god unto himself, and even with the atheist worldview, there is no room for god; the standard by which you call something good or evil is your god. The human *spirit, the lawmaker of the soul* in all of us, is how we will determine right from wrong.

When we are losing the battle to determine good from evil, our human spirit, *our God consciousness*, the means by which we determine something to be good needs to be redeemed or brought back to a place where we are able to know the difference. Jesus said it this way in John 3:6 (ASV), "That which is born of flesh is flesh and that which is born of spirit is spirit."

"And you will know the truth and the truth will set you free" (John 38:32, AMP).

The Christian worldview: sin and evil in the world. How we think about what life is supposed to be is the basis of faith in the Bible. It allows you to base your own opinion on what you perceive. Adversely, if will and fate are on a collision course with destiny, the atheistic worldview and the end result is the end of concise life as we know it. "Nothing to live or die for and no religion too." Then let's drink and be merry for tomorrow we die. This may be what you perceive life to be. But the Bible asks how did you come to believe that.

Is it by your own convictions or by whatever others believe for you? The substance of faith in the Bible is based on *how* we came to believe or perceive things to be, and its evidence determines *why* we believe. The truth about facts will only be revealed by actively seeking out these facts and allowing yourself to be a witness to their authenticity. Faith has evidence, but actively seeking it opens the door to the truth. This seeking is the natural progression of thinking and is the means by which we logically determine our opinion based on the truth. You can never know if you are a lottery winner unless you first buy a ticket. Second, you have to hold on to the ticket till the lottery is drawn, and third, look at the results to win. You may have a ticket, but if you don't hold on to it till the results are revealed or never bother to check the results, you can never know if you are a winner or not. And that's how many of us Christians and non-Christians treat Christianity. My pastor has a quote I like, "A faith that is not tested is no faith at all." So we as human beings owe it to ourselves to put what we believe to the test, Christian or atheist.

So how does the Christian worldview deal with the evils of this world? Where did it originate from, and is there an answer to how best to navigate life in the light of the effect that evil has on us as individuals?

The Bible calls evil sin. In a Christian worldview, sin came about by one act of rebellion from Adam, the first living being created in the image of God. And as the federalist view explains, "Like a nation gone to war, we all pay the price and share in the casualties." The Bible talks about a tempter who enticed Eve to eat from the forbidden fruit. But like most politicians, sorry, what was said was not the whole truth. It sounds great, but the devil is in the details. Sorry again. Is there a difference between a lie and a half-truth? In my opinion, yes.

A lie may be used out of self-defense, but a half-truth is sinister and intentional. So in the context of what the Bible calls the fall of man, the tempter, the sinister teller of half-truths, enticed Eve to sign up for something that was a bad deal, questioning God's promise seemingly because of her decision on something she knew little about because till then, there was no death, and because of Adam's choice, we as her children now have to die to self, questioning our decisions as we make our way through life. I have always been curious about the difference between a bad decision which leaves room for error, as in Eve's case, and a bad choice, an actual act of the will as in Adam's case. But I'll let God be the judge of that. And I'm sure I will get some men who will disagree with me, but I'll let their wives be the judge of that.

Questioning her on her own knowledge about the facts and her capability to make a decision based on the truth and judgment, he promised her something that wasn't his to give, being like God with knowledge, wisdom, and truth, and made sure the decision was hers, placing the blame squarely on her. Now Adam wasn't tempted; he made a willful choice. I guess if you know better, then you are responsible for your decisions.

Then Adam who should have known better instead committed the same trespass, placed the blame on her when confronted by God, and took the side of the accuser. It's no wonder women have a hard time trusting men. Just saying. When God was walking in the garden, he did not ask for Eve. He asked, "Adam, where are you?" Because I believe Adam should have known better. I'm sure Eve was counting on Adam to bail them out, but the fear of consequences, *since they now knew right from wrong*, overwhelmed him. Never having felt guilty before, he did not know how to excuse himself from its penalty. And neither do we.

Before she was deceived, Eve may have decided that God's love was greater than his being just, thereby limiting the full truth about his love for us. However, you can't have true love without truth and sacrifice because without the two, love is just a game.

If you are not truthful with the person you love and are not willing to sacrifice for your relationship, the relationship will fall apart. And it did. Whether God forgave them or not is not the issue. Forgiveness without boundaries is not the kind of love you would have for your children, is it? So they were banned from paradise and on a journey that would ultimately prove that God's love grows greater in the light of our bad choices.

The father of lies, as the Bible calls Satan, said that you will be like God knowing good and evil, a half-truth that usurps God's authority. Yes, we are created in God's image, but no, we can't know what he knows. Now what parent wouldn't want their children to be like them? Sounds good, right? But no parent would want their children to know what they know at forty-five if the child is five years old.

Their relationship with God was breached because they were now too smart for their own good. I always wondered what my mom meant by that. And from that point on, men would be made to question their own motives.

The Bible says that sin entered the world and death by sin. When we are unable to handle the reality of life, we act out of desperation, looking for some form of justification for why things happen that are out of our control. We search for a reason why or an excuse for why we are made to go through the evils of life, and in the process, life becomes less worth living, and that downward progression has taken even the best of us to the edge. A spiritual death has occurred, undermining our foundation of hope in mankind.

Some believe that because life is unfair, you might say that God is gracious in that he allows the end of life as we know it to bring an end to the suffering we are made to bear. Still today, half-truths and bad decisions have had devastating effects on the entire human race. The decisions we make in life have an effect on us and all those we are in relationship with. Their effects are inevitable, but the more we try to wish them away, our conscience, the gatekeeper of the soul, keeps us in that never-ending battle for truth.

Since we as human beings have decided we could do things better on our own, we have been left to our own devices. Look were that got us.

Adam's first son, Cain, killed his younger son Abel because of pride and envy. He was unable to make the right choice because of a tarnished view of God's love and sacrifice passed down from his mom and dad. Love has less to do with feelings and more to do with sacrifice. Love is a decision, and without sacrifice, it's just an offering. Cain gave an offering. Abel made a sacrifice. An offering asks for favor; a sacrifice asks for forgiveness. Adam and Eve had lost a child, had a wayward son, a broken family, never able to understand what the truth is about why these things happened. The fear of guilt was passed down from generation to generation, not understanding the justice of God's decision. I'm afraid that to some, this may sound all too familiar and has thrust some of us into the fight of our lives.

How many of us parents are fearful to be brutally honest with our children? Let me say that this is the product of a half-truth we believed a long time ago. Truth is an agent for change, but when there is sin involved, fear and indecision can push us into rash decisions. The anxiety, frustration, and of the fear of half-truths can be found in the fine print no longer plain to see. Life has gotten so convoluted, as they say, "The devil is in the details." The fear of making the right decision is more difficult today than when I was a child, and I'm afraid it's not going to end anytime soon.

Half-truths put a burden on us to determine what is true and what is not and splinters the facts, putting us in the position that was ultimately God's. We need the whole truth and nothing but the truth to get a grip on reality, but most of us like the movie quote say, "Can't handle the truth," because of fear and guilt.

We know our children are capable of making bad decisions, so we are careful about how much truth we want them to know about at different stages of life. And if they are not skilled in knowing right from wrong or are forced to make moral decisions at too young an age, things can go from bad to worse quickly. Yet today because of the internet and social media, our culture is forcing our children into making premature moral decisions. And if you don't help them make decisions on how life really is, the schools and universities are more than happy to tell them what they can expect life to be.

And so sin came into the world and death by sin. There is a hopelessness in the world today, the likes of which we have never experienced before. Read chapter one. And because guilt, a by-product of fear, has us in its grip, as imperfect beings we are unable to tolerate the consequences that are part of the human experience. If you are a parent trying to set a path in life your children can follow with confidence, it's hard to feel blameless when truth and circumstances collide, and you have to watch your child navigate his or her way around sin, knowing the answer to why life is unfair lies within the will of the individual to make the right choice. And you hope you have laid a firm foundation for how to handle the truth. We all want to offer our children hope for a full and rewarding life. But to do that, we have to be able to offer truth that brings hope and not despair. But without experiencing this firsthand, we are unable to. You can't give away something you don't have.

So the Christian worldview of how evil entered the world is that by believing a lie and making a series of bad choices *that we as humans have been making excuses, for since the beginning of time, as we know it,* we are paying the consequences for.

The Christian worldview, unlike the atheist worldview, explains where evil came from. And the story does not end there. What about God? Has he passed judgment on us with a death sentence? No, in fact, the Christian worldview has an antidote for evil. Soon after the fall of man, God promised mankind would be able to conquer sin through a Redeemer, a Savior, and that he would beat the deceiver at his own game, revealing the whole truth.

He promised Eve that through her seed, a man would be born to restore truth to her human family and that through her lineage, a Savior who was the way, the truth, and the life would restore the broken relationship between God and her children. A child would be born of God through her, without sin, the hope for all mankind, God's only Son who would conquer death and rewrite the fall of man by forfeiting his will and dying a sinless death.

Cancelling the debt of death because of sin, he died fulfilling God's justice the penalty for disobedience and was raised from the dead because of his righteousness. A just judge is unable to condemn a guiltless person. And if that person dies in his innocence, the truth about that death sentence demands an answer. Justice can never rest without truth. God's love for us is to know that truth was restored. He no longer will allow his children to suffer unjustly for the sin of believing a lie. If God is a righteous judge, he cannot allow the righteous to be condemned, not when the truth about evil is exposed.

Just as when we believed the half-truth, we were condemned to repeat our past, so now when we believe the whole truth about God's redemption, we are made righteous, free again to choose our destiny. But like the lottery ticket we mentioned above, you have to be in it to win it.

And you can read this story of redemption in the Bible from Genesis to Revelation as it unfolds. Some have called it the greatest story ever told. But to choose to believe it is what I call God's greatest gift—free will. So the question is, what will you believe? Every one you are in relationship with is depending on you to make the right choice, especially your children. Don't disappoint them. They deserve to know the truth, and when they do, their consequences will take second place to how they navigate life.

Indecision

Indecision in any relationship is a game stopper. In any sporting event when they stop the game because they are not sure what took place, the tension builds while they decide, whether their findings are based on the facts. But imagine if they never came back with a decision. The frustration of the fans would cause an uproar that would have some heads rolling, I'm sure. The frustration of indecision in a relationship is a form of abuse in many instances. However, on a personal level, this can be a means by which you can allow time to make the right choice. But when life demands an answer, indecision can be a game stopper. You can only fool yourself for so long and stay in indecision before you will be penalized, just like in the game we mentioned above. Life is filled with decisions, some trivial and some important, but to stay in indecision for any amount of time will cause a personality disorder.

Time will change your circumstance for better or worse, and without your input, it will lead you down the path of indecision, a place where you become a slave to the changing world around you if you let it.

With indecision, you are left to your own devices. In a court of law, when you say nothing in your own defense, it's to your own demise. The court will decide your fate with or without your input.

As I mentioned, Henry Ford said, "Whether you think you can or whether you think you can't, you are probably right." The modern version is to do something even if it's wrong. The truth of the matter is that we have no way of telling what the outcome of our decisions will be, and with the world closing in on us, indecision leads to fear. In his book *Integrity*, Dr. Henry Cloud explains that people who are in touch with reality and have what he calls an integrated character welcome change. It's like they can't live in the status quo. Knowing change is coming, they charge headlong and are not afraid of failing because they know how to lose well. As he explains, everybody loses, but people who lose well don't repeat their past. But people who are losers who never learn from their past are doomed to repeat it. Add indecision to the mix and the results can be crippling. Repeat this downward spiral a few times and it's no wonder indecision has invaded the lives of so many because of fear.

Fear

Fear is the enemy of decision. Fear is the number one reason people don't take risks. But the successful ones embrace reality, take risks, and become overcomers. As I mentioned above, our thinking is 70 percent negative. But people who take on the world and are not consumed by what could happen dive headlong into life, learn by their mistakes, lose well, and become some of the wealthiest, fulfilled, complete people on the planet. Why? Because they know fear is a liar.

An acrostic I like for fear is *False Evidence Appearing Real*. There is a new song by Zack Williams. It's called "Fear Is a Liar." Please allow me to quote some verses.

Fear Is a Liar

When he told you you're not good enough
When he told you you're not right
When he told you you're not strong enough
to put up a good fight
When he told you you're not worthy
When he told you you're not loved
When he told you you're not beautiful
That you'll never be enough
Fear he is a liar
He will take your breath
Stop you in your steps

Fear he is a liar
He will rob your rest
Steal your happiness
Cast your fear in the fire
Cause fear he is a liar
When he told you you were troubled
You'll forever be alone
When he told you should run away
You'll never find a home
When he told you you were dirty
And you should be ashamed
When he told you you could be the one
That grace could never change
Fear he is a liar
He will take your breath
Stop you in your steps
Cast your fear in the fire
Cause fear he is a liar.

Well, if the impact of these words have struck a chord in you, then you know the effects fear can have on people. I also find it both interesting and somehow revealing that Zack attaches an identity to fear, "He is a liar." Most people who are bound by fear have nothing to be afraid of. FDR once stated, "The only thing we have to fear is fear itself." If you are caught in fear and indecision and you are a Christian, just remember your consequences are in the hands of the only One who knows the truth about your intentions and the reason you feel the way you do. Trust him, and fear will never be able to lie to you again. "There is no fear in love; but perfect love casts out fear because fear hath torment. He that feareth is not made perfect in love" (1 John 4:18, KJ21).

Isolation

The effects of fear are devastating. And when you take on fear as your reason for not wanting to continue with the things in life that you need to respond to, you become a prisoner to your own lie. Like a ship without moorings, tossed to and fro at every whim of other people's opinions or of the everyday trials of life, no matter how big or small, we are left to the mercy of a will-less fate. Giving up hope of ever maintaining a stable balance in life, we crash into the rocks of indecision. My heart goes out to many homeless people who have allowed indecision and fear to take over.

No good advice can help a person paralyzed by fear. And if you feel helpless, like the song says, fear will rob your rest, steal your happiness.

When your identity is taken over by your circumstances and the half-truths of life haunt you, if you are a prisoner of doubt and fear, isolation is where you will live out your sentence. But take hope because fear is a liar.

After realizing the advice of others cannot help us, we say things like, "You just don't understand. You can never know what it's like to go through this," and you believe you are the only person on earth with these problems. If you begin to believe you are the problem and feel isolated, let me caution you to get help. Once you are isolated and left to your own devices without divine intervention, you are doomed to live a life without hope.

Believe it or not, isolation is where many of us hide from the things in life we don't understand because we tuck them away, only to have them rise up and confront us in different areas of life.

Well, I have always been amazed of how the Bible comes alive in times of indecision, fear, and isolation.

Listen to Proverbs 3:5–6 (AKJV), "Trust in the Lord with all thine heart and lean not onto thine own understanding, in all thy ways acknowledge Him and He shall direct thy paths." This passage is a lifesaver because it takes the burden of the decisions we need to make and put them on God who can be trusted. Trust is much easier than responsibility. It's like living a second childhood. We all need to trust that what we are doing with the things we are responsible for and the choices we make are the right ones. So trust God with everything you do, especially if the road you're on is not working; it can be as easy as a child finding the way home. Just remember to trust.

"There is no fear in love but perfect love casts out fear, because fear hath torment" (1 John 4:18, KJ21).

A quote from Joyce Myer Ministries says, "If you are afraid of facing a person or a situation in life, God's love can help you put your fears to rest."

"'For I know the plans I have for you,' says the Lord, 'plans to prosper you and not to harm you, plans to give you hope and a future" (Jeremiah 29:11, NIV).

The good news of God's love will break through the fear, bring clarity to indecision, and set the captive free from isolation. Many of us have isolated the problems we can't deal with because of fear and have allowed them to continue to question our integrity. They stunt our potential for growth in some areas of life that would otherwise be productive.

The effects of these insecurities are blind spots in our personality, hitting a wall in life, never being able to close the deal, leaving gaps in our relationships, leaving others to question why we are unable to take the next step, denying the truth, allowing others to make decisions for us, becoming complacent, and becoming addicted to anything that will fill the gap, to name a few.

The more perceptive and intelligent we are, the more these issues will be magnified. Some of the most famous, gifted, and talented people suffer the most under these idiosyncrasies because they are unable to release their innermost character, the basis for who they are, and in some cases, this becomes a death wish. Because most of these individuals will proclaim to be self-made, they need something greater than who they are to set them free from themselves, a higher power as some programs call it. But without a remedy and not just an emotional fix, these programs only cause the situation to become worse to those who are too smart for their own good.

The remedy is to answer the questions about ourselves that haunt us, to stand in the truth, and to have faith enough to believe that the truth is more powerful than the lie. If we could be rich enough in truth to buy back those things about ourselves that were pawned off for something that is a temporary fix, it is where freedom and redemption begins. But for that to happen, we need a Redeemer, someone who sees us as someone worth the sacrifice or the investment. And when we deal in truth, it will allow us to realize how much we need our self-worth to be bought back. When we allow the truth to change what we once thought about ourselves and let the past be a schoolteacher, the price that was paid for those who get a new start *redeemed* can never be taken for granted. Your conscience, the gatekeeper of the soul, the human spirit within us, will be free to begin again, the new life or like Jesus said, "Born again of the spirit," and that's precisely why we need God.

Chapter 8
The Redemption of the Human Spirit

The word *redemption* has a number of meanings, but its root meaning is Latin for *to buy back*. In a pawnshop, an item has a grace period in which it can be bought back. The item is pawned for its cash value at the time it is rendered. After a period of time, the items loan to worth value decreases, making the item worth less to the owner as time goes on. At one point, the price of redemption is not worth the value of the item. And it becomes the property of the shop. Generally speaking, items as little as ten dollars and well into the thousands of dollars remain on the shelf at pawnshops across the country for an untold amount of time.

But to the originator, the creator, or inventor who had an intention and a purpose for his or her creation is where any item's real worth is found. I have looked at some of the silliest inventions and said, "What the heck is this?" till I found its purpose. And I am reminded of that every time I look in the mirror.

I have always wondered what happens with the unclaimed dreams that seemed possible to us in times past, the hopes and dreams that were swept away in the never-ending busyness of life. For some, they remain like a remnant or a lingering flame of the hopes and dreams of a child. To others, they are a haunting memory of mistakes we have made that have robbed us of the purpose we are here for. The people, places, and things that have been there at our disposal, that would have made the difference in we being successful and fulfilled in who we were meant to be, that we by some twist of fate have allowed to slip through our fingertips, never to come our way again, pawning them off for something worth less than their original value. Life can at times ask us to trade off something of value that used to be for something that could be time worth spending for just spending time. And just like in that pawnshop, the loan to value decreases. When the things worth spending time on are pawned off for the things that just take time, their loan-to-worth value decreases, but their true value cannot be diminished.

The truth is, our lives need purpose, and along with the character we were born with, we need to be put into play with a plan to follow. Without it, we can never fully develop to our potential. Without a plan or direction, we are like vessels without a port of call, having enough wind to achieve our goal but no sail or rudder to guide us. Like a ship without moorings tossed to and fro with any wind of doctrine, as the Bible says, we look for any chance at hope for what may seem like an endless search for direction that can get us back on course to where we know are destined to be. We have what it takes, and we know where we should be going, but without direction, life becomes a never-ending search for the dreams we know need to be fulfilled to make our life meaningful. But no matter how old you are or how many times we go down the same dead end, run the same race, or come full circle only to land where you started, you are still you with everything you need to fulfill your purpose. You still have your personality, your character traits, and your talents. So it's never too late. And as long as you have breath, time is on your side.

To know how to use these traits properly is where we fail, and things get out of order. Everyone suffers from some sort of personality disorder when it comes to life. Young children have to learn to ask before being given something. The ones who are not taught this grow up to be impolite or maybe even thieves. So the order is to ask, and you will receive. The ones who are taught to be polite and ask will get much more out of life.

I've learned that a question before a comment works well with my wife. But when I have an opinion on something and I am looking for her input and I voice my opinion first, the communication drops off. Instead of just answering a question, she first has to judge whether my opinion is a valid means to an end. Just saying. There is an order to communicate properly. So getting things in order is a key to having our lives meet the time we live in and to stay relevant. The Bible says it this way, "A word fitly spoken is like apples of gold in pictures of silver" (Proverbs 25:11–13, AKJV). And just like the words we speak when we follow a plan and put things in order, the path we are on in life becomes easy to follow but not without purpose and value. When things are set in order, time and circumstance will be on your side. The things that are meant to be will fit into place, and time follows its natural progression. It's the nature of things to follow order. But when disorder is the issue, time cannot follow circumstance. When things are allowed to happen at the wrong time and circumstance, *the way things happen* collides with reality. It causes chaos, doubt, and the fear of the future. And words that are out of line can further the gap between purpose and circumstance.

Without the hope of getting back on track, we become a disorderly person, and when that hope is dashed to pieces, as we can see more and more today, many of our youth wind up paying the price.

Fulfillment in the things we do is a dynamic that can promote purpose and initiative and will give way for an individual to reach heights far beyond their expectations. But is rarely the case today.

Most of us, if we were honest with ourselves, would admit under the right circumstances that there is still hope for our fulfillment. Some of us are stuck in a cycle of life that holds the reality of who we were made to be at bay, chasing our dreams through a maze of broken, missed chances and lost opportunity, chasing that proverbial carrot, or looking for the end of the rainbow.

We may even realize that we are chasing a dream. But the things dreams are made of cannot be bought or sold for what their true worth is. They need to be redeemed and bought back by the original owner to understand their full value and purpose. Its true beauty is in the eyes of the beholder, but value and purpose are different.

Beauty is in the eyes of the beholder, but value and purpose are transferable.

Because of the busyness of our society, for a child to be held in their father's arms today has become a rare occurrence and one that most of us are unable to recall. But the value of a child's worth is beholden in their father's face. As a newborn is held in their father's arms, the value given by a smile or a silly gesture from their father imparts significance. The response to a father's love comes from the soul of a child no matter what their age. The authoritative love found in their relationship with their father offers a place of safety, a harbor of stability, and the assurance and hope of a fulfilling life. Their character will conform to the love and safety found by this bond of trust. Life becomes worth living, and value and purpose are transferred.

Even in their innocence with a newborn, the will to continue on and the approval of their father becomes a vital part needed for their maturity. The stability and authority of the love of a father for his children brings serenity and a confidence found only in their relationship. This significance becomes a part of who we are. To be a partaker in this transfer of value and worth is the missing piece for every person lacking confidence, self-worth, peace, and the purpose that will make you want to continue on with the hope of ever fulfilling life's dreams. There are some questions that can only be answered by a father's love and confidence in an individual. This value and confidence is a building block on which a person's character can stand and will be a reference point throughout life as to the direction they need to go. But without it, not knowing what the purpose that they were intended for can take them in many different directions.

However, when value and purpose are redeemed and bought back by its originator, their intentions are made clear. Since the beginning of time, every individual who has ever stepped into the world has asked the question, "What do I do next, or which way should I go?"

The direction they take and the decisions they make can be trying, tedious, and difficult without someone who has gone before them in life. It is human nature to ask a parent for direction. But to find one who can be a lighthouse for our journey in life is a true blessing. The father-child relationship was intended to be the force for good in the human spirit but has been lost to today's lack of fathers.

The missing pieces of life that leave us puzzled and are left unanswered need the wisdom of someone who can see us as an innocent child and with authority-instituted purpose, someone who will take responsibility for our being here, loves us and trusts in who we are without condition from birth until present and without any preconceived expectations, holds the key to open the door for us to find our purpose and significance.

A mother's love can change the world, but the input of a responsible father can not only make it possible; he makes it a reality that is attainable. A mother will always be there affirming your intentions and letting you know she knows you are that person you want to be. But a father lets you know you have what it takes, and you have everything you need to make it a reality. The plans set for you are what will lead you to fulfilling your destiny, and a father's assurance is what will allow us to stay the course.

The love of a mother is different than the safety of being held in the arms of a father, although the Bible describes the wisdom that the world was created with as sometimes in the feminine gender, and the encouragement of a mother's love is what is sometimes needed to push us over the edge. The direction and purpose found in the affirmation of a father's embrace creates a place of well-being and solitude that is lacking in our society. And like any sailor knows the wind and sails are needed to make the journey possible, without a rudder, we have no direction and are left to the mercy of the sea.

The lack of physical contact from a father has left some doubt about their role in the lives of children and in the family. And his absence in their lives, it leaves a gaping hole in the soul of an individual. Moms are always there to support us in our endeavors, but fathers are for the most part absent in the lives of many today, unless you happen to be one or the lucky ones. When someone is lacking in ambition, it takes a father to build confidence where it is lacking. Whether you are a boy or a girl, when at a young age you were involved in sports and you were at bat or you had the ball, how did seeing your father in the stands affect you?

A father's affirmation is what makes little girls feel beautiful and want to grow up to be women and little boys to be obedient for only one purpose— to gain their father's approval. Without it, these kids will grow up with the questions most of us still have. Who am I, and what am I doing here?

As a boy, the memories I have of being one on one with my father have impacted me in ways that have left me with indelible impressions that I can recall in vivid color by just closing my eyes. Though rare as they were, their impact on me are a powerful reminder of the influence that my father had over my life. His influence and approval had the authority to change the course of my life and define my value. Just a nod of approval by him was enough to make me the person I have always wanted to be and would give me the confidence to overcome even the greatest obstacles. The truth of the matter is that my dad was not there for me for the most part. But that never diminished the value of that relationship. I'm sure some of you can relate. If not, read on.

The approval of a loving father and the encouragement of a wholesome mother are the recipe for a successful future for any children in their care. And circumspectly, the respect given by their children give them the authority to take their role as parents. Unfortunately, this may sound foreign to some of my readers, but these transcendent truths are the foundation for a thriving and successful society.

Some of the most successful people in the world have had their father as their coach. Tiger Woods, at the age of five I'm told, under his father's guidance had been giving golf exhibitions, a view into the future of the pro golfer he was meant to be. Venus and Serena Williams whose father Richard's role has provided them with the platform he knew was what they needed to succeed. And the list goes on.

The fatherless epidemic of today has had a serious impact on our inner cities as well as the affluent communities across the country. From the gangbangers in Chicago to the overdose/suicides in Hollywood, many are attributed to the lack of a father role. Women love to be told that their beauty and their charm are irresistible and that they are a lifeline for the stability needed for life to reach its full potential. Their wisdom, although not always appreciated, if heeded can subvert many of life's difficulties. But their true beauty is multiplied in the arms of their father. The opinion of someone of the opposite sex is a key motivator for a woman, and acceptance without condition will pretty much make the world go round. *I love my daughters.* But the lack of dependability of fathers are a breeding ground for the abuse we see played out in life today. But let me say this, dads, it's never too late. There is nothing and no one that can take your place. The pieces left out in the life of an individual and the hole in their soul can only be filled by knowing the love and will of their father.

Boys can never reach their full potential without the consent and affirmation of a father. They will perform on life's stage for just about anyone for the acceptance that is desperately needed by their dad. Gangs know this when they are looking for recruits. They adopt these kids and accept them just as they are and understand their confusion with life. They let them know they are not the only one going through life having to fight for what they want. But they never let them know that the battle is within.

I will tell a story worth repeating. As an old Indian sat on a log with his grandson, he said to the boy, "Inside of us are two wolves, a good wolf and a bad wolf. And they are constantly fighting with one another. 'Which one wins?' asked the grandson. 'The one we feed the most' was the grandfather's reply." And that battle is fought in the life of every boy today, age being no barrier.

Men need to know that the battles they fight are not in vain. The war has already been won by those preceding them and is worth fighting for. The confidence to continue to fight for the right cause can turn an average boy into a hero. The success that he gains by adhering to his father's wisdom makes his father a legend to all those who come after him. Legends are never lost when men are found, a redeeming quality every father possesses.

Women will become valuable to themselves on two fronts—beauty and acceptance. They value themselves as being the lifeline to a civilized world. To know that not only do they have what it takes but that they are someone that is worth giving a life for will spark love and devotion, and that is what makes the Proverbs 31 women so attractive.

The love of a father will not only affirm beauty in a woman but virtue. The heart of a woman filled with glamour and excitement without virtue can be a long, disappointing road. But that virtue is formed by their beauty both inside and outside. A father can view both; most other men cannot. In times of distress, women sometimes need a lifeline or an anchor of truth that will support them and let them know that their heart along with their feelings are worth following.

To diminish a woman's feelings is to break the commandment that Jesus said was the second most important. "Love your neighbor as yourself." And judgment is swift when we break this one. And all the men said amen, unless you like being exiled with an emotional maze of questions that have no answer.

Our inner abilities are formed by the character traits we are born with and by the decisions we make along life's road. But without good direction by a loving parent, it's easy to get lost in ourselves and not be able to attain our full potential. Without a parent, we are left to the will of whoever will take interest in us. There are untold stories of how young people wind up in terrible situations, drugs, human trafficking, gangs, and homelessness due to the absence of a parent or guardian of good character and moral stability. But oddly enough, these statistics are not limited to those without good parents.

As the moral fabric and the foundation of the family is diminished, so are the hopes and dreams of so many of our young people today. And the disappointment of parents as their children's lives and future are dashed into pieces have become overwhelming for so many.

We as a society are trampling on the innocence of the childhood experience and forcing our children to make moral decisions before their time due to a lack of parenting and more so today a lack of fathers. Most single family homes are run by women, so it's no wonder that men are losing their credibility in the view of most moms and kids. I would have to say that there is less respect and trust for men today than any other time in my life. The percentages of men headed for moral bankruptcy, whether in or out of church, is alarming. I can't remember a time when more pastors have left the ministry due to a moral failure. Whether it's due to an accusation by a colleague or something that happened years ago, the diminishing creditability of men makes them an easy target for defeat. The most recent Me Too movement has exposed the irresponsibility of men when it comes to the respect for women. And to say that they have brought this on themselves is for the most part an understatement and in many cases true. I would never diminish the mistreatment of women young or old, but the real problem is we are feeding the bad wolf. The amount of sexually charged pornographic material has flooded the media and society to the point that the norm has become an enticement for men and women, young and old, and the acceptance of what may have been off limits five years ago is now not only accepted but required in order to be socially acceptable.

I know of teen girls who have mentioned to their parents that at the age of fourteen their friend was not sure if she wanted to keep her virginity by the end of the summer. When society puts a strain on the family, it's the men who need to live up to their character and the role of husbands and fathers; if not, it's just a matter of time before it will be "You Too." The value of the family and its redemption is in the hands of the fathers. To allow this trend to continue will be the beginning of the end of America as we know it.

As I sat in a dentist's office the other day, I watched a father interact with his daughter, and I was thrilled to see the sincere interest and openness that made their relationship so attractive.

I somehow knew that her ability to be open and honest with her dad was the foundation of who she knew she was. I was impressed by her dad's openness to agree or disagree with her without her being discouraged. Obviously, their relationship is founded on the acceptance and virtue needed by more fathers today. She found what most of us need, the peace and contentment of being in a safe relationship with our father and the transference of worth mentioned above that validates who we are.

The value of the human spirit is beyond measure. You can't put a value on happiness, contentment, significance, direction, encouragement, and the freedom to be who you are meant to be. The enormous potential that will be released is what makes people world changers.

But without a mother, the enthusiasm is lost, and without a father, there is no value in the pursuit of happiness. Life, liberty, and the pursuit of happiness can only have value with a loving parent, guardian, or mentor at the helm. If not, the journey can be long and tedious, especially for those with the perception to see life as it really is. It's true that the hand that rocks the cradle rules the world. And so the value and virtue of a child can be found in the face of their father.

To be able to look into your father's face and find acceptance and recognition is a vital part of how we handle the future. With the confidence and support of a father, fate and chance are second to success. Where hope and trust is at the helm, faith and significance follow. Success becomes the future, and life is full of joy and fulfillment. When circumstance becomes the servant of truth, the freedom to take risks is what makes people great.

Knowing your father is key, but having his approval is what makes greatness attainable. The love of a father for his children can calm the storms of life for anyone at any age. It can bridge any generation gap and bring relevance to any situation. It's prophetic in nature and makes dreams a reality. Think not? Just look at Jesus who fulfilled his Father's will and became the most prominent person to ever live.

These precepts are never governed by time. The longer the span of time between what was, what is, and what was meant to be only makes the hope of fulfillment grow exponentially. Everyone, no matter what our age, are waiting for our ship to come in—our fifteen minutes of fame, the break we have been waiting for, the winning lottery ticket, or hearing the words greeting, "Pilgrim, your search is ended" or "Well done good and faithful servant." However, the longing to be loved and accepted is the key to an individual's freedom to be all that they were meant to be. Without it, there will be times that like the lever of a pin-ball machine that puts the ball into play, our efforts and the obstacles of life are mainly left to chance. And the longer we play the game, the better we get. But life is not a game, and to be sent back only to be thrown into the game of chance in an endless cycle has consequences no matter how many points you score and can leave us hopeless in our pursuit of ourselves. Only until you know whose hand is on the lever can you find the faith and trust to continue. Your identity and purpose are in their hands, and their will for your purpose can only be made clear in who they are. The answer to a successful life is found in who you believe that is.

The Father's Will: Life's Purpose and Transcendence

The ultimate world-changing event has happened because of a Son's will to be obedient to his Father's plan for his life. Jesus had an earthly mother so we could have a heavenly Father. Have you ever asked the question why God chose his Son to be born of a woman? We all have an earthly mother, and we all have an earthly father.

Jesus, however, had an earthly mother and a spiritual father. And just like today, it seems everyone may have an earthly mother to relate to but not all earthly fathers are there even when present in our lives to influence us and give us what we need most.

I have always been amazed at the relevancy of the gospel. It's what makes it a living word, and without the obedience of a faithful Son, it could have no redeeming qualities that authenticate its truth, and the power it has when followed has changed the lives of the untold millions who have tapped into the fullness it brings to even the most destitute and hopeless who follow its precepts.

The obedience to his Father's will made what was possible practical. And with God as his Father, what was impossible was possible. To fulfill the will of his Father was Jesus's life purpose, and he chose not his will to be the course of his life but his Father's will. This one act of his will to be that of his Father has changed the course of history and is resident in all of us. The most powerful thing we possess is the will to choose. But who or what we choose to believe in will determine whether we are a success or a failure.

Where is the influence and integrity of fathers today that will impact the lives of their children in ways that will make them want to be all they were meant to be?

His faith in who his Father was is why through his obedience to his Father's will, his purpose in life, was fulfilled. The will to obey can be a springboard to success. The potential available in yielding to the greater good is what our character needs to find purpose and fulfillment. Because if who we are is all there is in life, the disappointments and the effects of trials and failures as time goes on will overtake even the best of our efforts and intentions and leave us alone and empty. But like the Bible, it says, "Obedience is better than sacrifice." To practice it is to tap into the peace and potential in life that passes all understanding.

If you are a father, the question is, do you have enough trust in who you are to be a guide to your children in the things in life that can convince them to trust you know what's best for them, to trust and be obedient to that purpose, and to be willing to give their lives for it if necessary? The responsibility of that position should bring godly fear in the heart of every father. The fact is, it's what every child is looking for, a purpose to believe in that they will stake their lives on. Instead, we see countless suicides and overdoses by both young and old that scream out, "What is the use of living a fruitful existence without purpose?"

His Father was not present with him on earth; nevertheless obedience to his Father's will is what fulfilled his destiny, made his life worth living, and gave him a purpose worth dying for. As Martin Luther King said, "A man that has not found something he will die for, isn't fit to live." The role of a father is a spiritual calling that not only fulfills a purpose for the child but makes a pathway for filling a void that otherwise would become a hindrance for the progression of life. It is not a physical role and has nothing to do with any particular race or bloodline. The male counterpart of a relationship is not what makes a father. Fatherhood is actually a relational choice. There are countless sex partners who have aborted their role as a father to search for themselves, children having children. No, fatherhood is adoptive in nature. There are hundreds of programs that are available today for any man willing to take a fatherly role in the life of a child who was abandoned by his mom's sex partner. If any of this makes you feel uncomfortable, it's your conscience; please pay attention to it.

The relationship between a heavenly and an earthly father as it relates to an earthly child is where a father's help for his children is found. It connects the life we live on earth to the purpose and virtue that transcends the time we live in. If we as fathers know and trust in the greater good, then transcendence will follow virtue to make the things that were impossible possible, and life takes on a whole new perspective. If you need to read that again, please do; it's worth it. I didn't get it the first time either.

Without Jesus being born of a woman and taking on the likeness of a man, feeling the emotional and physical pain of the human experience, our relationship to God would only be superficial. Without him being born of a virgin, we could never as human beings know who his Father is. And his heavenly Father would never be able to relate to the human experience with mercy and compassion, the missing link between God and man.

He is the only One who has ever seen his Father face to face. The transference of value and purpose given to him by this personal one-on-one relationship with his Father was what compelled him to complete the purpose he was here for. And so this transfer of value and purpose is available to all who trust and obey in God the Father. Being obedient to his Father's will was the hallmark of who he was, and that decision brought the love of God and the price of sin to the crossroad of salvation. If you are an American, you know the price of our freedom was purchased at great cost but not without obedience to a cause bigger than ourselves.

The Bible says that Jesus was the firstborn of the Father, full of grace and truth. The Holy Spirit was born with his convictions, and the reason he was here was to be all his Father wanted him to be. Those convictions transcend the purpose for a value-driven life. His purpose and value in life was there in him before he was born. And so the value of every human life was established in the human spirit in all of us before we ever leave the birth canal. A predetermined plan for our abilities, our talents, and our character traits are set in place with the same level of success available to everyone here today. The ultimate purpose of his existence was to make his heavenly Father available to the fatherless generation we see today. The adoptive quality of that relationship has become a life-transforming experience for countless millions of people throughout history and is the antidote for most of the tragedies we read about on a daily basis.

The power of his love for his Father drove his compassion to be all he could be in obedience to his Father's will. And so the Father's will over the life of a child has the power to make the ordinary into the extraordinary and is what gives ordinary people the ability to live a life of fulfillment and overabundance. His earthly mission was to do the will of his Father. And similarly to today, his Father was physically absent. Nevertheless, his ultimate mission in life was to be like his Father and to portray his Father's will by his every breath. He said, "The things you see me do, I do according to my Father's will." So what compelled him to do his Father's will even to the point of death? The value of who his Father was to him and the trust his Father instituted in him to carry out the will of his Father was the reason of his existence. The honor and trust that compelled him to carry out the will of the Father made him who he was, a transcendent truth available in every father-child relationship. Yet the will to choose was his alone, and so it is to all of us.

He found value in who his Father meant him to be. The power and influence of the truth of who his Father is and his Father's purpose for his life was revealed by his obedience even to the point of death and is what made his sacrifice so powerful but not only because he died in obedience to the Father's will, but he also died for all those seeking the truth about life. The truth is, his own people betrayed him, yet he clung to the will of the only One who mattered in his life; not counting the cost, he did not ask for justice to be served but only to be justified in the eyes of the only One whose opinion mattered. I guess it's easier to forgive your enemies when you learn to forgive your own family and friends who betrayed you. Just saying.

The pain of being betrayed by someone you love without having the will to forgive is a death wish to the spiritual well-being of many, Christians and non-Christians alike. But please allow me to minister freedom in the truth of what Christ did for you in sacrificing his will to do the will of God the Father. The innocence of the sacrifice had to be greater than the guilt of the offense for redemption to take place. Let me say that again. The innocence of the sacrifice had to be greater than the guilt of the offense for redemption to take place.

I hope you got that; if not, your conscience and the convictions that follow will not be satisfied. And the search for peace and rest for your soul will continue.

To die for a cause greater than themselves is what makes people heroes, but to offer forgiveness at the point of death to those who wrongfully accused you and to take your innocence to the grave is what Jesus did. And that one act where the innocent paid for the guilty had the power to change the course of men's lives and bring hope ever since man has had the hope to live for a cause worth dying for. For if he was God as he claimed to be, then God died for you.

For someone on death row who knows in their heart they are innocent, this is a reality they live with. The grief born out of the effect of the lies and hurts imposed by those we love is a soul stopper. Husbands, wives, children, parents, brothers, sisters, friends, and business partners are all too familiar with the loss of hope in our fellow man that these situations bring. Ultimately, the gospel message is founded on forgiveness for those who we love and cherish the most that have violated the trust of that loving relationship, as did the Jews and Jesus's closest friends. Without this message of forgiveness, love diminishes.

The effects of his obedience to his Father's calling on his life has changed the course of history and shifted the course of the lives of the most vile of men. Why? Because forgiveness is the most powerful force in the universe. It offers to trade forgiveness for offense and in Christ's case, innocence for guilt.

The value and virtue found in his life of obedience to his Father's will has and will forever be the standard by which the value of all human life is measured. Without the hope of his life, death, and resurrection, the value of human life diminishes with every tragic event that has come across the pages of history. The virtue in the saying "All gave some, but some gave all" would be lost without the hope in a greater good. The ultimate price paid for the emancipation of mankind in the sacrifice of one life for another is what we as human need to believe to be able to experience life to its fullest and to be redeemed from the hopelessness of a life lived without purpose.

The redemption of the human spirit was found in the value and purpose of his Father's love for mankind, and his sacrifice is what made it attainable. And so it is as Dr. Martin Luther King said, "If a man has not discovered something he will die for he isn't fit to live."

So if the exponential limitation of time cannot hinder the redemption of the human spirit and our will is to be obedient to the value of life, let us not grow weary in our pursuit of the value that our heavenly Father put on our life by transferring the value found in his Son to us. The value of his Son giving his life can never be lost but will only be found in you by the redemption of the human spirit. Thank you, and God bless you.

Appendix
A Collection of Poems by the Author

A Father's Help

In days of old when dads were bold and walked with good intentions
The children's hearts turned toward that light they saw in clear dimensions
So doctors, lawyers, artists came, some worked their hands in wood
And on the land and ore the sea they spoke of brotherhood
Across the sea to lands unknown the hope these dads instilled
Was told by those who knew it best for that cause some were killed
And so it was throughout this land these dads were all called father
The children stood up for that right with glory, blood, and honor
But now that time has walked on by these dads today still fight
They fight with moms they fight with kids you see they lost their right
Oh they still harbor good intent their walk is not the same
Instead of honor, blood, and guts they look for who to blame
For kids that curse and moms that weep they say it's just my luck
And years are spent in toil with hopes to buy them with a buck
But all the tea in china couldn't get them what they need
They need a light they need a hope they need a noble deed
Oh things are nice yes things are good but there's just an offering
You see things were not made or meant to make an anthem ring
In God we trust it's written on our currency you say
But would your children trust in God if He were you today
So listen, dad, please be a man don't look the other way
Please help your son accept and want to be a man one day
It's okay to admit you're wrong it's just the price of honor
Give of yourself reclaim that ground they really need a father.

A Christmas Poem

For God so loved the world that He gave His son you see
So me and mine and you and yours can be filled with Christmas glee
And joyous songs and trees and gifts that's only just a start
But I can't help but wonder what was on the Father's heart
As on that day He gave to us His only Son begotten
Oh I'm quite sure that He knew then our sins would be forgotten
I wonder if He saw our kids' eyes shining 'neath the tree
Or did He then turn toward His own to think of Calvary
Well maybe He had hoped that the Babe's glory we'd behold
But then again He must of known what the prophets had foretold
Without the pain for He is God He saw right through the end
But could He give this precious gift without a heart my friend
At that His own received Him not His heart they mocked and spurned
As broken bruised tattered and torn His gift to Him returned
So then where are the heart and thoughts of God on Christmas day
Are they on the joy we share or on the price He paid
Or could He still have gifts untold things eyes have never seen
Like peace on earth good will toward men beyond man's wildest dreams
Could God the Father be so big He sees right through the grins
The joy, the laughter, peace, and hope and praise we lift to Him
And sees a day when man will see not through this dark glass dim
The joy of Father with His Son and those He freed from sin
And then before the heavenly hosts are all the earth proclaim
That we from Zion come with song for whom the Lamb was slain
To take back all our foe has spoiled and see love's seed restored
To walk again in fellowship with God our King and Lord

To Whomever

Once upon a time or a time that should have been
I had had no senses no feet no eyes no skin
I had not even place of mind no story thought could tell
Neither was there space on earth made for my lifeless cell
Then on a day when time was full He called me son or daughter
And said He too one day like me was lead a lamb to slaughter
Well He's my Father now I know no matter what my size
But for the life of me can't tell why tears still fill His eyes
When He calls a name I never had and yet I understand
That He's my Father and He's got the whole world in His hands
I often want to ask Him why my name's not Jack or Jill
Mary, Judy, James, or Bob, Michael, Tom, or Bill
But just before I get to ask I look upon His face
And realize that His love for me's worth more than time or space
Although some say I have no name well one you'll never know
I've heard it said that there's a place where I'm called baby doe

Mary Had a Little Lamb

Mary had a little lamb His fleece was white as snow
And everywhere that that Lamb went He let the people know
That through the love and grace He shared that He could set them free
But they led Him up a hill one day when He was thirty-three
There Mary cried the angels wept and even heaven sighed
But even so in just three days the Lamb was glorified

Friendship

A friend in need is a friend in deed
And needs help friendships grow
And friends won't count your humanness as either con or pro
A friend is there to listen
In that safety they'll confide
In trouble times you'll know them 'cause they're always side by side
Loose or win through thick or thin
They'll never count the costs
Their faith will stand to move God's hand
They'll make your gain their loss
Now friendship is a hallowed place
Where truth and grace abound
A place of hope and safety
It's where the lost get found
And when life's narrow path has room for just one and no other
Just let them know that there's a friend sticks closer than a brother

Death/The Way God Loves Us

As I thought about death I realize
It's lawless
It's unfair
It's always unexpected
It's unpredictable
It can overtake you if you let it
It doesn't look at gender
It don't care how good you were
It don't ask if you're old enough
It's shameless
It's naked compared to the truth
It won't allow you to make excuses
It's senseless
It's there even when you don't want it to be
It's inescapable
It don't care if you're two or a hundred and two
It can't be excused
It's relentless
It's a soul stopper
It don't ask questions
It don't need an answer
It changes the way you live your life but isn't that the way God's love is toward
us
It changes the way you live your life
It don't need an answer
It don't ask questions
It's a soul stopper
It's relentless
It can't be excused
It don't care if you are two or a hundred and two
It's inescapable
It's there even when you don't want it to be
It's senseless
It won't allow you to make excuses
It's naked compared to the truth

It's shameless
It don't ask if you're old enough
It don't care how good you were
It doesn't look at gender
It can overtake you if you let it
It's unpredictable
It's always unexpected
It's unfair
It's lawless

"Jesus said to Martha at the tomb of Lazarus, 'I Am the resurrection and the life. He who believes in Me, though he may die he shall live. And whoever lives and believes in Me shall never die.' Then He asked, 'Do you believe this?'" (John 11:25–26, NKJV).

CPSIA information can be obtained
at www.ICGtesting.com
Printed in the USA
LVHW030055070120
642672LV00021B/578/P